MW00861010

INGENUE TO ICON

Howard Vincent Kurtz

Trish Donnally

with introduction by Nancy Rubin Stuart

INGENUE
TO ICON

70 YEARS OF FASHION FROM THE COLLECTION OF MARJORIE MERRIWEATHER POST

Hillwood Estate, Museum & Gardens, Washington, D.C.
in association with D Giles Limited, London

© 2015 Hillwood Estate, Museum & Gardens

First published in 2015 by GILES
An imprint of D Giles Limited
4 Crescent Stables, 139 Upper Richmond Road,
London, SW15 2TN, UK
www.gilesltd.com

Library of Congress Cataloging in Publication Control Number: 2015005283

ISBN (hardcover): 978-1-907804-40-3
ISBN (softcover) 978-1-931485-06-7

All rights reserved

No part of the contents of this book may be reproduced, stored in a retrieval system, or transmitted in any form or by any means, electronic, mechanical, photocopying, recording, or otherwise, without the written permission of the Trustees of Hillwood Estate, Museum & Gardens and D Giles Limited.

For Hillwood Estate, Museum & Gardens:
Kate Markert, Executive Director
Liana Paredes, Director of Collections and Chief Curator
Howard Vincent Kurtz, Associate Curator of Costumes and Textiles
All images, unless otherwise noted, are from Hillwood Estate,
Museum & Gardens

For D Giles Limited:
Copyedited and proofread by David Rose
Designed by Alfonso Iacurci
Produced by GILES, an imprint of D Giles Limited, London
Printed and bound in Hong Kong
All measurements are in inches and centimeters;
Height precedes width precedes depth.

Front cover: *Marjorie Merriweather Post* ca. 1935
Photograph: John Alfred Piver
Frontispiece: Detail of fig. 104 *Majorie posing for Frank O. Salisbury painting,*
New York City, ca. 1934

CONTENTS

Foreword

Marjorie Merriweather Post (1887–1973) lived an extraordinary life. She was born in the nineteenth century, came of age in the beginning of the twentieth, and lived through both the Roaring Twenties and the 1960s. She embodied in many ways the extreme transformations of those eventful decades that were especially relevant to the evolving status of women, reflected in the fashions of the time.

Marjorie played many roles throughout her long life. As the only child of entrepreneur C.W. Post, she learned the ways of business when her father took her as an eleven-year-old girl to board meetings where older gentlemen discussed the major issues facing the Postum company. Afterwards, her father expected her to be able to summarize the discussion and weigh in with her own opinion about what direction they should take. In her twenties, she inherited the company she knew so well and became one of the richest women in America, although it was not until she was in her late forties that she was allowed officially to join the board. She learned as a young woman how to direct a large household staff and she had a long history of inspiring others through her generous charitable giving. Always, she was very conscious that how she dressed both amplified her role and reflected her own personality.

Throughout the decades, Marjorie's clothing reflected her keen interest in current fashion trends. She started out emulating the Gibson Girl as a demure eighteen-year-old Edwardian bride in yards of lace and leg of mutton sleeves. Later, she and husband E.F. Hutton were the "it" couple of the twenties, entertaining in New York, Palm Beach and the Adirondacks, always in the most up-to-date fashions, for day wear as well as elegant dinners and fancy dress balls in the evening. When she married diplomat Joseph E. Davies in 1935, she became "ambassadress" and representative of the U.S. government, with all the wardrobe gravitas that position demanded. Always the epitome of style and grace, Marjorie was keenly aware that her parties, movements and fashions would be duly charted and reported by the press throughout her lifetime.

In 1957, at nearly seventy years old, Marjorie Merriweather Post established Hillwood as her primary residence and planned that it would be left as a public museum. She filled it with her magnificent collections of Russian Imperial and French eighteenth and nineteenth century decorative art. Luckily for us, all during her long life she treated her clothing as a serious collection as well, preserving and documenting it. Thanks to her vision, Hillwood has a singularly complete and exquisite repository of costumes and accessories, a rich resource to study the development of American style, the changing role of women in the twentieth century and one woman's journey from a young, fashion-conscious ingénue to an assertive and iconic grande dame.

Howard Vincent Kurtz's excellent catalogue and its accompanying exhibition chronicle seventy years of Marjorie's life. Nancy Rubin Stuart, author of the Marjorie Post biography *American Empress* contributed an insightful introduction. Fashion writer Trish Donnally offered a valuable outsider's point of view and editorial guidance to the project. We are most appreciative of the Marjorie Merriweather Post Foundation's support for these efforts. There is such a wealth of material that the exhibition reflects the seasons, showing spring and summer fashions first, then changing over to fall and winter. The book is divided into four riveting sections, each providing context for Marjorie Merriweather Post's transformation from *Ingenue to Icon*.

Kate Markert
Executive Director
Hillwood Estate, Museum & Gardens
Washington, D.C

Acknowledgments

I am delighted to share the story of Marjorie Merriweather Post's public and private lives through the lens of fashion and the study of her personal costume collection at Hillwood Estate, Museum & Gardens. I hope to demonstrate to the reader her standards of beauty and elegance and those of an age that no longer exists, from her exquisite wedding trousseau to glamorous beaded dresses, custom-made special occasion ensembles, and complex designer gowns. As objects that delight the eye and stir the imagination they are worthy of preservation and study of their own and as expressions of Marjorie Post's infinite sense of style. She knew that her clothing could be viewed as a snapshot of costume history and saved her collection for display at Hillwood. Her collection represents some of the best designers, latest trends, and most exquisite materials from the 1900s until the time of her passing in 1973. Her life and story are sewn into the seams of every garment.

Ingenue to Icon is the result of the cooperation and collaboration of many people. A sincere heartfelt appreciation to the Post family women, especially Marjorie's daughter Dina Merrill Hartley, granddaughter Ellen MacNeille Charles, and granddaughter Nina Rumbough, who shared delightful, humorous, and touching stories of mother and grandmother.

At Hillwood, my great thanks go to the Marjorie Post Foundation, board members, staff, and volunteers who shared their enthusiasm and vision for this endeavor, in particular: Kate Markert; Angie Dodson; Audra Kelly and her staff; Judith Paska and her staff; Lynn Rossotti; Kristen Regina; Margaret Huang; MJ Meredith; Ren Wuang; Estella Chung; Manuel Rouco; Manuel Diaz; and the late Anne Odom. Many thanks as well to project interns Gina Guzzon, Nora Carleson, Elizabeth Lay, Morgan Blattenberg, and Katie McLain.

My deepest gratitude goes to Liana Paredes, Hillwood's Director of Collections & Chief Curator. Without her support and mentoring this project would not have happened.

For their editorial contributions, I particularly express my gratitude to Nancy Rubin Stuart, the biographer who brought Marjorie Post's story to life, for her Introduction to this publication. My sincere appreciation and gratitude goes to Trish Donnally for her incomparable dedication and collaboration during the writing process.

I am thankful to my colleagues at George Mason University and The Costume Society of America for their camaraderie and eagerly shared knowledge. Finally, to my husband Howard Jaffe, extended family, and dear friends, I am grateful for their sustained support throughout the creation of this project.

It has been my sincere pleasure to research and write about one of the most remarkable and fabulous grande dames of the twentieth century. As Marjorie's youngest daughter, actress Dina Merrill, said "Throughout her life, Mother maintained her classic style and elegant manner of dressing. She had a style that was all her own."

Howard Vincent Kurtz
Associate Curator of Costumes and Textiles
Hillwood Estate, Museum & Gardens
Washington, D.C.

INTRODUCTION

BY
NANCY RUBIN STUART

A Youthful Initiation

Marjorie Merriweather Post, a pioneer who left a legacy of accomplishments in business, art, social, and even diplomatic circles, also left a remarkable wardrobe lovingly collected over seventy years. Presented in the following pages are the handmade dresses, gossamer gowns, magnificent hats, and exquisite jewels that defined Marjorie's inimitable style.

Even as a child growing up in Battle Creek, Michigan, Marjorie loved clothes. At an early age, her mother, Ella Letitia Merriweather, taught her to wield a needle and thread and before long Marjorie was sewing clothes for her dolls. Her father, Charles William, known as C. W. Post, had a different influence upon her. By the late 1890s he had developed his coffee substitute, Postum, into a major food industry. Fearing that when grown, Marjorie might be manipulated by unscrupulous employees, he decided that she learn the intricacies of the Postum Cereal Company. He insisted that Marjorie attend corporate board meetings after school. He would later grill her on what was discussed.

By the time Marjorie was nine, C.W. took her on business tours to cities like Detroit, Chicago, New York, and New Orleans. As heiress to the Postum Cereal Company, Marjorie had to look the part. Consequently, C.W. ordered her fashionable dresses from Chicago and New York. During the summer father and daughter also traveled together to Newport and Paris. That exposure undoubtedly heightened Marjorie's early acquaintance with high style.

Education and Presentation to Society

By 1901, C.W. traveled so frequently to Washington, D.C. on business that he bought a home on Vermont Avenue. Determined to introduce his adolescent daughter into society, he enrolled Marjorie in the Mount Vernon Seminary, a fashionable finishing school. Marjorie's mother Ella, who was estranged from the restless C.W., also moved into a nearby apartment on M Street.

Although distressed by her parents' divorce, Marjorie described her Mount Vernon years as happy ones. "I adored it [the school]," she recalled years later, "because I had so many girls of my own age to be with and it was all a new experience." By her mid-teens Marjorie had become a tall beauty who loved clothes so much that her father cautioned her to be discreet about her spending. "You have more than double the clothes, shoes and stuff that *any girl* no matter how rich should have at 17."

From the Midwest to the East Coast

In July 1905 Marjorie announced she planned to marry Edward Close, a recent Columbia Law School graduate from Greenwich, Connecticut. Her letter brooked no argument. She had, after all, just turned eighteen years of age.

C.W. Post holding his baby daughter, Marjorie
Fort Worth, TX, 1889

Previous page:
Marjorie Merriweather Post Davies at Tregaron
Washington, D.C., ca. 1950
Photograph: Yousuf Karsh

Marjorie Merriweather Post
New York City, 1905
At age 18, Marjorie posed for this studio portrait in the latest winter fashions, an Edwardian ensemble accented with dramatic hat and ermine muff.

"Be very sure your heart tells you that Eddie is the one," C.W. replied, "He is lovely and we like him very, very much, but he must be all to you." Of course if she was certain, "I shall be just as happy for you as I possibly can be."

On August 31, Ed Close purchased an engagement ring at Tiffany's. While less wealthy than the Posts, Marjorie's fiancé was a member of the Brevoort family, descendants of the Knickerbockers who had owned land in prerevolutionary Manhattan. In contrast to the "old money" or the so-called "Four Hundred," the Posts were considered *nouveau riche*, a fact that Marjorie either did not sense or, if she did, ignored.

The awkwardness of the elder Posts' divorce and the illness of Ed's mother led the couple to decide upon a small wedding. In compensation, C.W. told Marjorie she could buy anything she wanted for a trousseau. Immediately, she began shopping.

The wedding was to take place on December 5, 1905 in the chapel of Manhattan's Grace Church, between Tenth and Eleventh Streets, in honor of the Brevoorts' early roots. Marjorie's satin wedding gown was stunning, embellished with lace, trailing orange blossoms, and a waist knot of rhinestones and pearls. Two wedding presents—diamond earrings from C.W. and a diamond sunburst necklace from Ed worn over a strand of pearls—would frame her face.

The night before the ceremony something happened that profoundly changed Marjorie's life and approach to fashion. As she walked down the aisle during the wedding rehearsal, two women from the Close side sat gossiping in a pew. "Well, she's a cute little thing considering who she is and where she's from," one of them sneered. Hurt, rage, and a desire for revenge ripped through the bride. As Marjorie recalled in a conversation with her son-in-law Cliff Robertson, "I'll show those SOBs if it takes me sixty years." Someday Eastern high society would understand that Marjorie Merriweather Post was a woman to be respected, a ground-breaking businesswoman, a generous philanthropist, and a grande dame decorated by no fewer than six foreign governments, who was every bit as admirable as those from the old-line social register.

Soon after their marriage the newlyweds moved to Battle Creek where a disappointed C.W. learned that his son-in-law Ed had no interest in becoming the heir-apparent to the Postum Cereal Company. By 1908 the young couple returned to Greenwich. There Marjorie birthed two daughters, Adelaide Brevoort Close in July 1908 and Eleanor Post Close in December 1909. Photographs from that era reveal her outfitted in Edwardian frocks and hats as befit a proper prewar young lady.

To their Greenwich friends, the Edward Closes epitomized glamour. Ed, who had resumed his law practice in Manhattan, was considered a model of patrician propriety and Marjorie admired as a stylish spouse who dwelled in a two-winged, eleven-bedroom mansion, The Boulders.

Two events soon intervened. The first was C.W.'s suicide on May 9, 1914, which left his shocked daughter Marjorie the major shareholder in the Postum Cereal Company. Although Ed served as the "official" board member, she assumed behind-the-scenes responsibility for

major decisions. To facilitate management of the company, the Closes moved to Manhattan. There they rented a Beaux Arts townhouse on East 92nd Street and within a year purchased it. Marjorie began thinking about herself as a businesswoman.

On April 6, 1917, the United States entered the Great War and Ed Close was drafted. At thirty years of age, Marjorie was thus compelled to assume new responsibilities. Among them were war-related problems with shipping and finding substitutes for the corn and wheat used in Grape-Nuts, Post Toasties, and other Postum products.

Passionately patriotic, she knitted sweaters for the soldiers and funded an entire Army hospital in France. By the time Ed returned from the war, he and Marjorie had grown apart. Moreover, with imminent passage of the Nineteenth Amendment, independence was in the air. To Ed's consternation, she filed for a divorce. Once it was granted, he returned to Greenwich and soon remarried.

Marjorie with her aunt,
Mollie Post
Battle Creek, MI, 1915
Marjorie and her beloved Aunt Mollie relaxed together at Calmary Farm, Battle Creek, both wearing light flowing summer dresses.

1920s Wealth and the Jazz Age

Inevitably, Marjorie's assistance to the Postum Cereal Company board of directors increased her sense of power. As a New Yorker, she regularly attended the opera and the theater and studied at the Metropolitan Museum of Art with the British art dealer Sir Joseph Duveen. At thirty-two, Marjorie was beautiful, sophisticated, and conversant with the principles of big business. Several years earlier at a Long Island dinner party, she met the legendary stockbroker, Edward F. Hutton, then married to Blanche Horton. In 1919, Marjorie bumped into him again and learned that he had become a widower. A passionate love affair followed and on July 7, 1920 Marjorie and E.F. Hutton wed.

Ned, as Marjorie called Hutton, soon became involved with the Postum Cereal Company. In 1922 he listed it as a public offering on the New York Stock Exchange. A year later, as the chairman of the company, Ned moved its headquarters from Battle Creek into a Manhattan skyscraper. In 1926, Postum began acquiring products such as Jell-O and Maxwell House coffee. At Marjorie's insistence he also purchased Birdseye Frozen Foods in July 1929 and renamed the company General Foods Corporation.

In contrast to her first husband, Ned embraced the high life. It was, after all, the dawn of the Jazz Age, an era inspiring freedoms from old traditions, a moment when being "smart" and "sassy" replaced "proper" and "respectful," when "display" was preferred to "discretion," and a time when café society—celebrities, entertainment, and sports figures— were attracting more attention than the "stuffy" members of high society.

As money poured into the coffers, Marjorie and Ned indulged in the era's lavish lifestyle. In the early 1920s they purchased several large properties. Among them was a Tudor estate on Long Island (later C.W. Post College), Hutridge, a 207-acre summer "camp" on Upper Saranac Lake in the Adirondacks, and a fifty-four room triplex in Manhattan. The crown jewel was the 1926 construction of Mar-a-Lago, a palatial Hispano-Moresque home on seventeen acres in Palm Beach.

Marjorie at her winter home, Mar-a-Lago
Palm Beach, Florida, ca. 1927
Photograph: Townsend Studios
Marjorie is seen here at Mar-a-Lago in casual slacks, the kind of garment she wore exclusively for sporting and resort activities.

Marjorie also adopted the clothing of the Jazz Age. Appearing in sleek flapper-style dresses, fur stoles, and cloche hats, she looked a decade younger than in her Greenwich days. She also hosted dozens of balls, dances, and galas in New York and Palm Beach. Among them were costume balls in which she appeared in dazzling jewels, gowns, and wigs dressed as her favorite character, Marie Antoinette.

In June 1929, Marjorie Merriweather Post Close Hutton achieved a long-awaited triumph over high society. In London, outfitted in a dress of cream and green organza embroidered with rhinestones, her left shoulder adorned with a Cartier pendant of cascading pearls and diamonds, her ears sparkling with diamonds once belonging to Marie Antoinette, Marjorie was presented to a smiling George V and Queen Mary at the Court of St. James's.

Transformation and The Great Depression

The Great Depression sent shock waves through Marjorie. No longer would she spend money on ball gowns, costumes, or extravaganzas. An heiress now grown thoughtful about wealth and poverty, she stored her jewels in a safety deposit box. With funds saved from the insurance, she financed a soup kitchen for women and children in New York, the Marjorie Post Hutton Canteen.

By 1931, Marjorie sponsored benefits for the Samaritan Home for the Aged and the Judson Health Center and served on the Gibson Unemployment Relief Committee. She even stood on Manhattan streets during rush hour soliciting money from the employed. In reflection of that era, Marjorie often appeared in tailored suits and dresses reflecting the glamour of Hollywood, which was becoming a pacesetter for fashion.

To escape the public animus towards the wealthy, and to ensure their youngest daughter Nedenia's (later known as the actress Dina Merrill) safety in light of the recent Lindbergh baby kidnapping, Marjorie, Ned, and Dina spent six months during the years 1932–34 aboard their 316-foot sailing ship, the *Hussar V,* visiting Europe, the South Pacific, and South America. Nautical life necessitated still another change in Marjorie's wardrobe. Shorts, light shirts, sun hats, and even native tropical dress replaced the dresses and suits worn on shore.

The human tragedies of the Depression weighed so heavily upon Marjorie that she was soon advocating the social policies of Franklin Delano Roosevelt. Ned vehemently objected and soon they were engaged in bitter quarrels. He had become a womanizer and in 1935, after being caught sleeping with a member of Marjorie's house staff, she without hesitation filed for divorce. A year later Ned relinquished his position as chairman of General Foods. Disillusioned by the divorce, Marjorie longed to have more control over her father's old company, and by 1935, she had become a member of the board of directors of the General Foods Corporation.

By 1935, such a position was finally attainable, albeit only for a small, select group of American women. Henceforth, Marjorie would serve tirelessly on the board. Insistent upon

her father's high standards for excellence, she routinely collected samples of General Foods products while traveling and reported her findings to the board.

In 1936, *Fortune* endorsed the heiress's new position and reported that Marjorie was "altogether conversant with the corporation detail." That new status provided still one more incentive for a muted clothing style. At board meetings for General Foods, she appeared in stylish business suits, their sole embellishment a pin or a strand of pearls.

Marjorie and Nedenia aboard Hussar IV with a giant tortoise 1930 Even dressed casually in sportswear in the tropics, Marjorie still wore gloves.

Although she was devoted to the company, Marjorie did not lack for male companionship. While at a Palm Beach dinner party, she met a 58-year-old international attorney named Joseph Davies. Discovering they had similar political views, they spent the evening talking. A resident of Washington, D.C., Joe had long been married to Emlen Knight and was the father of three grown daughters. To his eldest, Eleanor Tydings Ditzen, it seemed that Joe had been struck by lightning. "The guests were having cocktails in the garden and Marjorie came in and down the stairs and that was it," she reminisced.

Washingtonians were outraged over Joe's divorce and his plans to marry Marjorie. On December 15, 1935, the smitten bride, dressed in a peach velvet gown whose color matched an enormous wedding cake and a thousand chrysanthemums, became Mrs. Joseph Davies. Twenty months later her new husband received a call from President Roosevelt's office. Joe was to become the ambassador to Soviet Russia under Joseph Stalin.

Marjorie was horrified. The country was remote, its climate harsh, and its politics hostile to Western democracy—a far cry from the glamorous appointments she had hoped for in Western Europe. Nevertheless, the post had an exotic appeal, which would elevate Marjorie's status to that of an ambassadorial wife with a hardship assignment.

In preparation for Russia's bitterly cold winters, she ordered her tweed coats lined with chamois for extra insulation and left many of her jewels in a safety deposit box in the States. Nevertheless, once Marjorie and Joe were settled at Spaso House (the American ambassadorial home in Moscow), her clothes dazzled fellow ambassadors, Russian dignitaries, and their wives. The Soviets, recalled Marjorie's daughter Dina, "were absolutely goggle-eyed. They'd never seen anything like it." The Communist mentality of the 1930s had long since discouraged displays of wealth. Consequently Soviet women did not wear high-style clothes, jewels, or other fashion accessories.

Among those entranced by Marjorie's clothes was Paulina Molotova, the wife of the prime minister, who hosted a luncheon in her honor. "Marjorie has made a great hit with the wives of the Communists here," Joe wrote Eleanor Roosevelt after that event.

By the end of March 1937, Marjorie and Joe had charmed the Soviets and the United States Department of State reassigned them to Belgium. After the September 1, 1939 Nazi invasion of Poland, the American government ordered all ambassadorial wives home. During her years in Soviet Russia, Marjorie collected Russian art, antiques, icons, and Fabergé and once home, became a sympathetic spokesperson for the peoples and culture of Russia.

Marjorie, Joseph E. Davies, and Emlen Knight Davies on their way to the Soviet Union
Berlin, Germany, 1937
Ambassador Joseph E. Davies, flanked by Marjorie (right) and his daughter Emlen Knight Davies (left), strolled in Berlin.

The overseas sojourn also taught her a critical lesson. Regardless of conflicting political loyalties, clothes speak their own language.

As a young woman, Marjorie used fashion to highlight her beauty and attract suitors. At age 46, she had returned to the city where she was educated with an important new perception. Style was an adjunct to the social power she would soon wield among the movers and shakers of Washington, D.C.

Post-War and the Cold War Era

The war years bolstered Marjorie's status and now for the first time, the press praised her as a Washington hostess with incomparable clothes and jewels. In 1941, while hosting a diplomatic reception for Maxim and Ivy Litvinov at the Davies' rented Foxhall Road mansion, an awed reporter from the *Washington Post* noted that she was "smartly turned out in a full-skirted frock of grey taffeta, set off with inserts of net in a leafy pattern—all very lovely." That same year after Joe's book, *Mission to Moscow* became a best-seller, he and Marjorie became nationally prominent and their photographs splashed upon the nation's newspapers.

Diplomatic galas were only one aspect of Marjorie's activities. As she had during World War I, she volunteered for the American Red Cross and donated the *Hussar V* (by then renamed the *Sea Cloud*) to the U.S. Navy as a convoy ship in the North Sea.

In the spring of 1942, Marjorie and Joe moved into a twenty-acre estate in Northwest, Washington, D.C. where they showcased their Russian art collection and hosted a Soviet-American congress, ambassadorial dinners, and charity benefits. By war's end Marjorie was consequently acknowledged as one of Washington's social arbiters, a hostess whose invitations to the powerful and would-be powerful were a sign of political favor. To young congressional wives like Lady Bird Johnson, an invitation to the famous hostess's garden parties was "one of the most glamorous things that happened every year."

Weary of traditional dinners followed by ballroom dancing, Marjorie decided to change her entertainment style to include "round and square" dances—ballroom dances alternated with square dances. The latter with its fast pace, group spirit, and the amusing caller pattern, was an instant icebreaker in the politically intense atmosphere of the nation's capital. Over the next two decades, innumerable politicians, diplomats, and dignitaries hopped, shuffled, and do-si-doed at Marjorie's square dancing parties in D.C., Palm Beach, and at her Adirondacks camp. To enhance its casual atmosphere, she appeared in colorful petticoats, skirts, blouses, and shoes.

Marjorie also sought to improve Washington, D.C.'s lackluster cultural life. In 1950, she hosted a garden party on behalf of the National Symphony, served as the honorary chair of the symphony's first benefit ball, and by 1956 had funded "Music for Young America," enabling the nation's visiting high school students to attend concerts. Simultaneous with her divorce from the bitter, and by then politically unpopular Joseph Davies, Marjorie was becoming known as The Duchess of the District of Columbia.

Marjorie and her dog, Scampi
Hillwood, Washington, D.C.,
1968

Marjorie's Public Persona

Having resumed her maiden name, Marjorie Merriweather Post purchased at sixty-eight years of age a large Georgian Colonial estate on twenty-five acres near Rock Creek Park and renamed it Hillwood. Filled with Beauvais tapestries, Sèvres porcelain, eighteenth-century French furniture, Russian icons, Fabergé, and paintings, the estate was the perfect setting for "the most fabulous hostess in all America," hailed *The Washington Star.*

Maintaining that "wealth is a greater responsibility than a privilege," Marjorie served on numerous corporate boards and organizations, funded a building for the Mount Vernon Seminary and Junior College, generously contributed to the Boy Scouts of America, became a founding member of the Washington National Ballet Foundation, and made anonymous contributions to the future Kennedy Center for the Performing Arts. Enhancing her stature were Marjorie's stylishly tailored suits, dresses, and gowns, designed by her favorite dressmakers.

Inevitably, her glamorous appearance attracted suitors, among them a handsome Pittsburgh widower, Herbert May, the soft-spoken executive vice president of Westinghouse Air Brake. Dashing, witty, and popular, the silver-haired executive often attended Washington parties and, like Marjorie, loved to dance.

The first time Herb brought Marjorie home to meet his adult children, his daughter Peggy expected an elderly woman. "I was totally undone. Marjorie was wearing an off-shoulder, form-fitting evening gown, and the Russian imperial emeralds," she recalled. 'My first impression was 'Dear God, when I get to be that age, let me look like her.'"

After the Mays married on June 23, 1958 at her daughter Adelaide's home in Maryland, in the weeks following the wedding, the couple had two receptions, one in Pittsburgh and another in Washington, D.C.

Marjorie and her Legacy

Perhaps Marjorie had a romantic blind spot. Or perhaps as Adelaide said, she simply had "bad luck", but whatever the cause, by 1963 Marjorie's marriage to Herb May ended. Even so, she refused to dwell in sorrow for long. On October 5, 1964 Marjorie appeared for the opening night of the Washington Ballet "Looking youthful and charming in a short evening gown...with a new escort," as *The Washington Post* reported.

During the winter of 1964–65 she entertained forty guests at Mar-a-Lago and spent the rest of that decade hosting charity teas, educational groups, and art lovers there and at Hillwood. Intending her Washington, D.C. home to become a museum after her death, Marjorie allowed as many as five hundred people to tour it each week.

Marjorie Merriweather Post and Colonel C. Michael Paul at the Red Cross Ball
Palm Beach, Florida, 1967
For the event Marjorie wore a set of diamond and turquoise jewelry, including an historic diadem that once belonged to Empress Marie Louise.

As a septuagenarian, Marjorie's silver hair, glittering jewels, and stately dress were regal. "Mrs. Post, at 78, resembles a Dresden doll, but gives the strong impression of being woven of steel wire. Her step is firm, her stamina discouraging," wrote the editors of *Life* magazine in 1965.

In February the following year, *The New York Times* described Marjorie as a woman with "patrician features" beneath which hid a "salty down to earth manner." The following February *Time* magazine stated that "At 79, Marjorie Merriweather Post Close Hutton Davies May is still slender and pridefully erect—but she is far more than merely a remarkably handsome woman...she is a grande dame of high society."

Dozens of honors and accolades continued to pour in. On March 15, 1967 when she turned 80, the National Symphony devoted a concert to her, which concluded with a "Happy Birthday" serenade. For Marjorie, becoming 80 was a time for consolidation, contemplation, and renewed charitable contributions. Distressed by the duration of the Vietnam War, she donated funds to organizations supportive of veterans and hosted garden parties for men from the Walter Reed Army Hospital and the Bethesda Naval Hospital.

Marjorie also continued to donate to needy individuals and contributed generously to organizations, including the World Wildlife Fund and the Palm Beach Fine Arts Festival.

Still lovely, Marjorie often appeared in gowns, furs, and tiaras in newspaper stories on fashion or beauty. She was dubbed "The Queen of Palm Beach" and "The Duchess of Washington, D.C." and was considered one of the most iconic women in the world.

On her eighty-third birthday, Marjorie hosted ninety people for dinner at Mar-a-Lago, after which guests were invited to participate in a round and square dance. Among the guests was syndicated columnist Suzy, who wrote that their hostess looked "like a hundred million...as she whirled and dipped in the tango...her pleated red taffeta petticoat flashed and her red shoes twinkled. Wow! ... Mrs. Post may well be the world's most beautiful and remarkable octogenarian."

Three years later, Marjorie Merriweather Post passed away, leaving a lasting legacy of enormous accomplishment. Her classic style, feminine grace, dignity, and glamour are reflected in the fascinating and sumptuous clothing she collected over a span of seventy years, as featured on the following pages.

CHAPTER 1

AN AGE OF INNOCENCE AND INDEPENDENCE

1903–1919

Fashion reflects the art of living and Marjorie Merriweather Post's spectacular wardrobe, collected over seven decades, provides tantalizing insights into a life of exceptional elegance and style. Marjorie grew to be director emerita of the General Foods Corporation in an era when women seldom worked outside the home. She assembled one of the finest collections in the world of rare Russian Imperial *objets d'art* as well as a superb collection of Sèvres porcelain. Châtelaine to several magnificent properties, including Mar-a-Lago in Palm Beach, Camp Topridge in the Adirondacks, and Hillwood in Washington, D.C., she traveled by private railcar, yacht or plane from one estate to another. Marjorie also became a highly respected philanthropist. Along the way, she collected a beautiful wardrobe spanning from 1903 to 1973. Think Gibson Girl wasp-waist ensembles, *Titanic*-style empire gowns, bugle-beaded chemises, bias-cut satin sheaths, and décolleté ball gowns designed to complement exquisite jewels.

Marjorie's distinctive upbringing gave her a unique perspective that no doubt influenced her inimitable sartorial style. Born March 15, 1887, the only child of Charles William (C.W.) Post and Ella Letitia Merriweather Post, she spent most of her childhood in Battle Creek, Michigan, where she had the rare opportunity of attending board meetings with her father who, after struggling with poor health, invented Postum and Grape-Nuts and founded the Post Cereal Company. C.W. was known to take his young daughter with him on business trips throughout America and abroad.[1] Exposed to the world of business, finance, and manufacturing as few girls in the late 1800s were and reminded often by her father, whose success continued to grow exponentially, that his company would one day be hers, Marjorie thrived on the attention her father showered on her and the entrée into his world that he shared.

Just as her father was teaching Marjorie the foundations of business, her mother was educating her on the intricacies of domestic life. Marjorie said of her mother:

> She was a marvelous needle-worker and made a great many of my clothes, especially the underwear. They were all trimmed with lace, little ribbons that were run through, etc. I would see her sitting there near her worktable for many hours of the day. When I was at the right age of course I was taught to do hemstitching, catch-stitching and to make all sorts of things.[2]

Even her extended family, her Aunt Mollie, the wife of Carroll, C.W.'s brother, and her paternal grandmother were teaching intricacies of good workmanship, which is a foundation for fashion. As Marjorie said:

Previous page:
Marjorie Merriweather Post posing for a studio photograph
Washington, D.C., 1903

1
Marjorie Merriweather Post at five years of age posing for a studio photograph
Battle Creek, Michigan, 1892

Aunt Mollie was a marvelous needle-worker and taught me embroidery and all sorts of things. Grandmother Post used to visit every summer and she taught me to knit when I was about seven, because she wanted me to make garters for her. These were a yard long and an inch wide and she wound them around the top of her stockings, turned it through; it was the regular plain knitting, it wouldn't come undone and it would hold.[3]

Growing up, Marjorie often emulated her mother's feminine ways, perusing her fashion magazines, including *Vogue, Harper's Bazaar,* and *Collier's,* and striving to follow her footsteps on the dance floor, where Ella was a natural.[4] Marjorie was keenly aware of her mother's style:

First and foremost, she was the most beautifully groomed woman, very small, very erect with a lovely figure … I think they used to tease her when she was first married, telling her that she had swallowed a poker as she sat up so straight.[5]

2

Marjorie Merriweather Post
ca. 1903
Marjorie was attending the Mount Vernon Seminary, a fashionable finishing school for girls.

Like mother like daughter, Marjorie would come to be known for her perfect posture as well.

Reared as a Christian Scientist, Marjorie generally eschewed drinking and smoking and made sure she got eight hours of sleep each night. "(Christian Science) has been the strength and comfort all my life," she said.[6] Leading a healthy lifestyle only enhanced Marjorie's natural beauty.

Making a transatlantic crossing at age thirteen with her parents, one of many times she traveled to Europe while growing up, Marjorie attended the grand 1900 Paris Exposition, her steamer trunks filled with dresses, hats, and shoes for the adventure. The *Exposition Universelle* with its Art Nouveau architecture included fascinating exhibits, depicting the latest in technology and luxury, such as the *Grande Roue de Paris,* which remained the world's tallest Ferris wheel for ninety years, talking films, the *Palais de l'Electricité,* diesel engines, moving sidewalks, and the opening of the first Paris Metro line. Among the most popular exhibits was the display of French fashion, presented under the presidency of renowned fashion designer Madame Jeanne Paquin. Her committee for this presentation included, among others, the Worth brothers and Callot sisters.[7] The following year, at fourteen, Marjorie left her midwestern roots and moved east to attend Mount Vernon Seminary, a private finishing school for girls in Washington, D.C., where she studied from 1901 to 1904. Her class of approximately sixty included daughters of senators, congressmen, and industry leaders. Just as her circle of friends grew, so did her confidence. Her interest in dancing increased during this time as she was attending Naval Academy dances in Annapolis, Maryland, often chaperoned by her mother, who had moved to Washington, D.C. to live near her daughter.

Joining the "modern drama" group at school, Marjorie also discovered a theatrical flair, participating in school productions, often playing the male role in an all-girl cast, because at five feet seven inches she was among the tallest in her class.[8] Her father had established the Post Theatre in Battle Creek in 1901, fulfilling his dream of bringing drama and music

3
*Marjorie Merriweather Post's Sweet
Sixteen portrait*
Washington, D.C, 1903
The two-piece evening dress
is a creation of the Baker sisters.
Marjorie celebrated her birthday
in Washington, D.C.

to the citizens of their hometown.[9] Marjorie often integrated the
drama and pageantry of the stage into her personal life through
her costume balls in the 1920s and other spectacular soirées in her
homes.

In the summer of 1902, C.W. swept Marjorie off to
England, joined relatives and took a stagecoach, complete with
a driver, four horses, and a liveried footman on an excursion to
Stonehenge and Wells Cathedral.[10] Marjorie later recalled:

> There never in the world was a trip that was more fun
> … We'd make about twenty-five miles a day … and as
> we would approach a village or town … the boys with
> the horns would announce our coming so that the traffic
> would give way …"[11]

When small groups of boys would appear in the streets to gawk and stare, the Posts would
toss them coins. On that fairytale trip, Marjorie and her father also attended the coronation
of Edward VII.[12]

Later that year, Marjorie penned a letter to her father on November 22 from The Willard
Hotel in Washington, D.C., thanking him for the beautiful diamond solitaire earrings and
matching ring he had given her and describing the experience of having her ears pierced:

> Dada,
> It didn't hurt much but after it was all over I had gotten up to leave and I nearly
> fainted, got hot, then cold and everything turned black & green. Some way they
> got me into a cab that came along and I gradually got over it. When I got home my
> clothes were just wringing wet with perspiration. The Dr. put black silk threads in my
> ears and I had the time of my life sliding them back and forth. At present when the
> earrings are not in I wear a piece of a whisk broom … Thanks for the lovely earrings.
> I feel so 'High Life' when I wear them.
>
> [signed] Budge[13]

Opposite:
4
Detail of fig. 5
In 1903, when Marjorie pinned a
handwritten tag to her Sweet Sixteen
birthday dress before packing it
away, she began to document her
fashion collection, which would
ultimately span seventy years.

5
Sweet Sixteen evening dress
White spotted tulle, ivory silk taffeta,
cream silk velvet, coral beads, clear
rhinestones
Baker, Washington, D.C., 1903.
48.8.1-2

6
Marjorie's Mount Vernon Seminary Senior Portrait
Washington, D.C., 1904
Marjorie wearing the ruffled pink dress in fig. 7 for her portrait.

7
Reception dress
Pink silk lawn, pink organza, pink chiffon, off-white silk taffeta, off-white silk ribbon, salmon silk ribbon
Bergdorf Goodman, New York City, 1903–04
48.24.1-4
This youthful gown, with graduated shades of pink and delicate bands of pleated silk ribbon, exemplifies high-end fashions from Bergdorf Goodman, a luxury retailer that Marjorie patronized from the early 1900s through the 1960s.

8
Detail of fig. 10
This dress was saved with a note for its special significance.

9
Petticoat detail of fig. 10

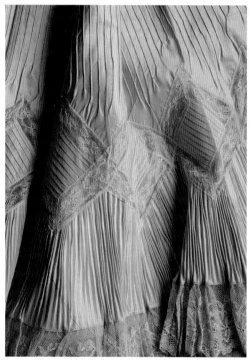

After her move to the East Coast, Marjorie's wardrobe grew significantly, partly because she loved clothes and also because as a fashionable young woman, she was expected to change as often as four times a day, more if she were involved in sporting activities. Marjorie needed dresses, coats, blouses, skirts, and sporting clothes that could carry her through mornings spent at home, afternoons of shopping or visiting, dinner parties, dances, balls, and sporty outings. Marjorie began shopping at Bergdorf Goodman in 1902, initiating a relationship with the department store that would last the rest of her life (see figs. 6, 7).[14]

The following year, 1903, the lovely young ingenue celebrated her Sweet Sixteen birthday in style wearing an Edwardian, two-piece evening dress created by the Baker sisters, who had a small dress shop in their home in northwest Washington, D.C. When Marjorie pinned a tag to the gown with a handwritten note marking the occasion before packing it away, she was starting her fashion collection, which would evolve and eventually reflect seventy years of beautiful fashion design.

By 1905, Marjorie exuded the essence of the Gibson Girl, the beautiful, modern and independent woman created by American pen and ink illustrator Charles Dana Gibson in the 1890s. Gibson's vision of this "New Woman," publicized in *Life* magazine, remained dominant through much of the first decade after the turn of the century in America and England.[15] Marjorie, who was confident, well-traveled, educated, and financially carefree, embraced the Gibson Girl's feminine look, which included shirtwaist dresses for day and high fashion gowns for evening, and a tiny "wasp-waist." The Gibson Girl was often described as "S-shaped," the curves in the front of her bodice sometimes enhanced by ruffles on her corset cover and a little bustle in the small of her back.[16] She wore her hair upswept, often secured with tortoiseshell or oriental combs (see figs. 13, 14).

10
Afternoon dress
Pink silk taffeta, pink silk organza, cream lace, pink silk chiffon, bone
Unknown Maker, American, 1903
48.14.1-2
Marjorie wore this dress the night she became engaged to Edward Bennett Close.

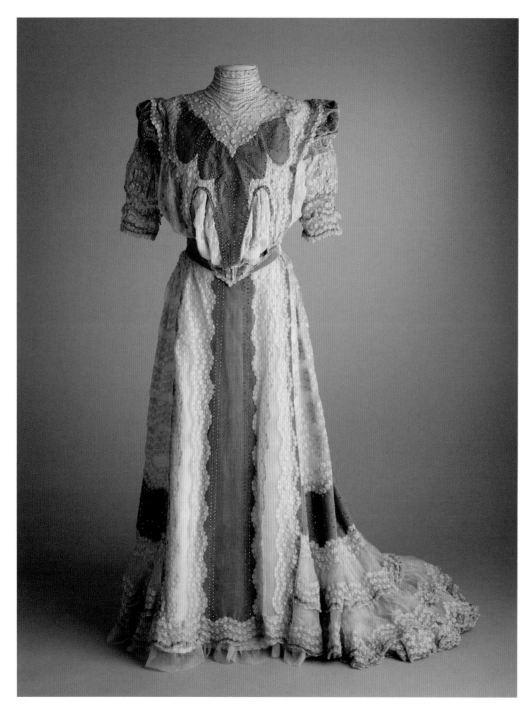

11
Afternoon dress
Blue-grey silk velvet, organza, lace, metal beads
Stéphane, Paris, 1903–4
48.6.1-4
Marjorie may have acquired this two-piece dress, a creation of Parisian couturier Stéphane, through one of the several American stores that imported French fashions. It is typical of the early Edwardian period in its ornamentation and structure with its studded metal beads, light organza bands and a filled neckline with a high stand collar of contrasting lace.

12
Evening dress
Yellow silk crêpe, silk taffeta, satin ribbons
Jay's Limited, London, 1903–5
48.7.1-2
This style was appropriate for evening wear when young ladies shed their high-collared, long-sleeve dresses. Marjorie wore this gown to a dance at the Naval Academy in Annapolis, Maryland.

13
Marjorie Merriweather Post seated at a writing desk
1905
Marjorie was the epitome of the Gibson Girl: confident, educated, well-traveled, and independent.

14
Gibson Girl drawing
Charles Dana Gibson
Collier's Weekly, November 29, 1902
Charles Dana Gibson (1867–1944) was an American graphic artist, best known for his creation of the Gibson Girl, an iconic representation of the beautiful and independent American woman at the turn of the 20th century.

Being fashion conscious, Marjorie likely would have worn a straight-front corset fitted long over the hips and laced snuggly in the back, because corsets were an essential part of a woman's wardrobe, even a young woman's wardrobe, during the Edwardian era.[17] Marjorie's love of lace may have grown around this time as well, because women were passionate about lace and lingerie just after the turn of the century. As time would prove, corsets remained a core part of Marjorie's wardrobe throughout her life, and her fondness for lace never diminished.

When Edward Bennett Close, a young lawyer from Connecticut, proposed to Marjorie, her father told her she could purchase anything she wanted for her trousseau, encouraging her to "make it as lovely as possible."[18] Meanwhile, Marjorie saved the dress she was wearing that evening in July 1905 when she got engaged and later added a handwritten tag noting the occasion. She and Ella had a lovely time together shopping for her trousseau, buying everything she needed for her wedding celebration, honeymoon, and related travel. Later, in the 1960s, Marjorie reminisced:

15
Marjorie and Edward Bennett Close
on their wedding day
New York City, 1905

16
Wedding dress
White silk satin, silk organza, open
cutwork lace, grosgrain ribbon,
rhinestones
Hitchins & Baleow, New York City,
1905
48.10.1-2
A magnificent mélange of white
silk satin and organza trimmed with
point d'angleterre lace, Marjorie's
wedding gown is embellished with
silver tissue, rhinestones, faux pearls,
wired lilies, and leaves of cotton floss.

(I wanted) the most glamorous wedding gown you could think of … I had a lot of
fun in New York with mother, selecting the whole trousseau. Of course the dresses
in those days were so elaborate with all sorts of feminine this and that. We went to
a firm called Hitchins & Baleow, which was a very successful and well known large
house. When I heard what they were suggesting I was fascinated with it.[19]

Her lavish trousseau included "dozens of dresses from New York's finest stores as well as nine
ball gowns, eleven pairs of boots, and six sets of lingerie," among other pieces.[20] Marjorie
described her dresses as being embellished with "miles and miles of handiwork, either in
embroidery [or] ruffles." Naturally, Marjorie also purchased lovely chapeaux, trimmed in
lace, velvet, and ostrich feathers, which were *de rigueur* at the time.[21] In anticipation of her
nuptials, her mother had purchased sublime sets of bridal lingerie in Paris for Marjorie a
year earlier.[22] In the early 1900s, lingerie played an essential role in a bride's trousseau and it
was traditional for young brides to begin marriage with many corsets, corset covers, garter
belts, and petticoats (see figs. 15–19).[23]

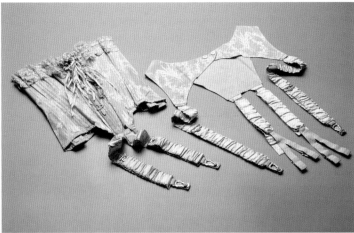

17
Detail of fig. 16

18
Wedding corset and garter belt
Attributed to B. Altman & Co.,
New York City, 1905
2014.5.1 & 2014.5.3
Part of Marjorie's trousseau,
the bride wore these the day she
married Edward Bennett Close.
The pieces are adorned with
delicate lace, a ribbon rosette,
and cascading ribbons.

19
Wedding corset cover and petticoat
Attributed to B. Altman & Co., New
York City, 1905
2014.5.9.1 & 2014.5.9.2
Part of Marjorie's trousseau.

Marjorie married Ed on December 5, 1905, at age eighteen, in Manhattan's Grace Church, her short sleeve wedding gown and train laced with *point d'angleterre*, rhinestones, pearls, intricate embroideries, and orange blossoms.[24] Her left opera glove folded back over the ring finger so the groom could slip the wedding ring on, because of course, no proper young lady would remove her gloves in public at the turn of the century. The couple spent their honeymoon at the Homestead Hotel in Hot Springs, Virginia.[25] Years later, Marjorie recalled:

> [t]he going away outfit was really something. It was a wine colored cloth: the main body of the dress was cloth, but up around the waist there was lovely lace dyed the same color as the dress, it was very elaborately arranged in the waist. There was a beautiful coat to it, almost full length. There was a strange little crescent-shaped opening, and I remember I put a five cent piece into it the day I was married and I think it is still there.[26] (see figs. 20–22)

Returning from their honeymoon, Mr. and Mrs. Close moved into their new home, The Boulders, a magnificent gift from Marjorie's father, complete with stables and a lake in Greenwich, Connecticut. A young lawyer's wife now, Marjorie was living in a haven for East Coast millionaires with some of the best-known and wealthiest industrialists, businessmen, and politicians as neighbors. William Rockefeller and his two sons, for example, lived in Greenwich at that time.[27] Marjorie was expected to socialize frequently, attend and host parties, dinners, philanthropic events, and artistic performances. With her new responsibilities, she began to buy more elegant clothes from Parisian couturiers and fine department stores, including Callot Soeurs and Au Bon Marché as well as high end custom fashion houses in New York City.

20
Traveling suit
Maroon wool, maroon velvet, ivory lace, maroon satin ribbon, bone, metallic gold thread
B. Altman and Co., New York City, 1905
48.11.1-3
Traveling suits were an important part of a well-to-do woman's wedding trousseau. This three-piece maroon wool suit with intricate detail in satin and lace was a special order to B. Altman & Co., a fashion retailer located at Sixth Avenue and Nineteenth Street, then New York's famous Ladies' Mile. Marjorie wore this suit while traveling by train to her honeymoon destination, Hot Springs, Virginia.

21
Traveling suit boots and stockings
Attributed to B. Altman and Co., New York City, 1905
49.99.1-2
2012.4.1-2
These boots and stockings were dyed to match her traveling suit.

22
Detail of fig. 20
The lace blouse includes intricate workmanship.

23
Nightgown
White cotton lawn, lace, satin ribbon
American, ca. 1905
48.25
This nightgown features an
embroidered monogram of "MMP"
on the front, just left of center.
Cotton lawn and other sheer white
fabrics were the preferred textiles for
sleepwear at the turn of the century.

24
Dress gown
White cotton lawn, white lace, pink
cotton silk ribbon
American, 1905
48.26
The gown closes at the center front
with a delicate pink ribbon.

25
Visiting dress
Peach silk and cream silk lace, cotton cord, peach silk taffeta, peach silk cord, wood
M.A. Boucicaut for Au Bon Marché, Paris, ca. 1910
48.91
Suggesting the exotic decorative influences of the Middle East and Africa, this dress is embellished with spiraled cording, and covered wooden buttons. Visiting dresses were designed to be politely subdued and modest in style and ornamentation.

26
Detail of fig. 25

27
Purse
Maker Unknown, ca. 1910
Silk, metal and seed beads
49.16
Seed beaded purses were a popular women's accessory at the turn of the 20th century.

28
Detail of fig. 27

29
Evening dress
Yellow silk taffeta, grey silk organza,
green cotton embroidery
Maker Unknown, ca. 1911
48.21
This evening dress has a boned
bodice, tulip shaped sleeves, and
a formal evening train. The high
waist announces a changing trend
in fashion.

30
Detail of fig. 29

Opposite:
31
Evening dress
Turquoise silk moiré, turquoise
cotton moiré, orange/gold silk
crêpe, orange tulle, turquoise/gold
silk cotton floss, turquoise/gold silk
ribbon cord, beading
Callot Soeurs, Paris, ca. 1907
48.22
Purchased from the Parisian
couture house Callot Soeurs, this
high-waisted evening dress in sheer
turquoise moiré over an intense
orange-gold silk skirt is heavily
embroidered with decorative motifs
and embellishments.

32
Detail of fig. 31
The Callot Soeurs label sewn inside
Marjorie's evening dress.

33
Detail of fig. 31

In Greenwich, Marjorie was managing a household staff of fourteen and almost sixty on the grounds crew.[28] At summer's end, her father requested an accounting of all monies spent. When Marjorie came up four pennies short, he told her to recheck her figures. She eventually found her error and accounted for every cent.[29]

A few years later, Marjorie gave birth to her first child, Adelaide Brevoort Close, on July 26, 1908. Eleanor Post Close arrived the following year on December 3. Marjorie and Ed, who were living a relatively quiet life in Greenwich, began vacationing in Palm Beach, Florida in 1909.[30]

Meanwhile, the winds of change were blowing through fashion. Hats almost took on a life of their own, piled with ribbons, feathers, and all kinds of embellishments, as their brims grew wider and wider. Dresses were getting looser, more ornamentation began to appear on shoes and stockings as hemlines began to rise, and parasols were prevalent. In Europe, bohemian dancers including Isadora Duncan, Mata Hari, and Loie Fuller were mesmerizing audiences with expressive dance, lightly veiled in flowing fabrics.[31] They inspired leading designers, particularly Paul Poiret, to begin eliminating petticoats and—most shocking—corsets.[32]

34
*Marjorie and daughters Adelaide
(left) and Eleanor (center)*
ca. 1910

35
Traveling dress
Purple linen-backed velvet, ivory
lace, jet beading, boning, bright pink,
silk satin
Widoff, New York City, ca. 1910
48.5
Marjorie owned multiple dresses
from designer Ellen Widoff, a
dressmaker in New York City. Like
the designs of many other fashion
houses of the time, this custom dress
displays remarkable craftsmanship in
design and luxurious fabrics such as
velvet, lace, and satin.

36
*Hat to complement traveling dress
in fig. 35*
Maison Maurice, ca. 1910
2012.9.9
This large, wide-brimmed hat,
decorated with feathers, typifies
a popular style of Edwardian
millinery. Marjorie paired this hat
with matching purple velvet shoes
and spats.

37
*Shoes and spats to complement
traveling dress in fig. 35*
Maker Unknown, ca. 1910
49.88.1-4

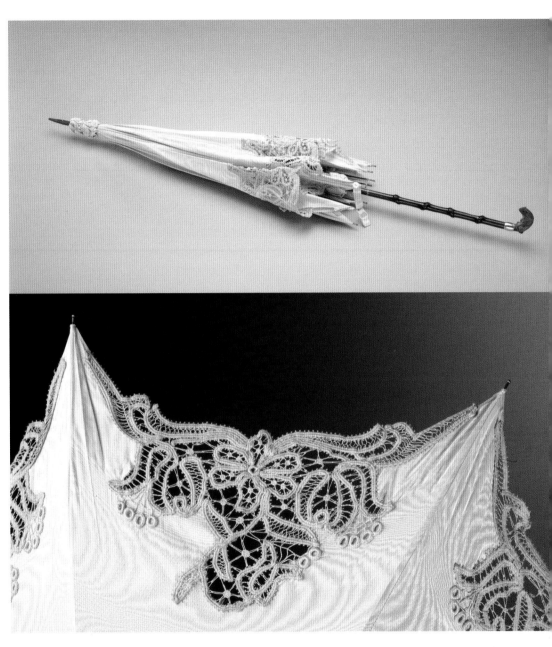

38
Rat Tail Parasol
Silk moiré and Battenberg lace
Maker Unknown, ca. 1910
2014.11.13

39
Detail of fig. 38

40
Lingerie dress
White cotton lawn, white cotton embroidery
American, ca. 1912
48.17
This dress, with its white-on-white motifs, was worn over a contrasting colored undergarment. The embroidered iris motifs were appropriate for garden parties and other outdoor events in the late spring and summer.

41
Afternoon dress
Pale pink silk, cream silk lace, lavender silk organza
American, ca. 1912
48.31
This elegant Edwardian afternoon dress features a hobble skirt, a fashionable Parisian novelty characterized by a restrictive skirt with a very tight, narrow bottom hem.

42
Evening dress
Light blue silk lawn, tan silk organza, tan cotton lace, tan silk net, pink silk organza, light blue satin, pink satin ribbon, clear bugle beads, faux pearl beads, boning, rhinestones
Widoff, New York City, ca. 1912
48.30
This evening dress is illustrative of the lavish adornment found on Edwardian fashions in the early 1910s. It points to Marjorie's changing taste from subdued colors and delicate embellishments towards bright silks, satins, and bold floral embellishments.

43
Detail of fig. 42

Marjorie's life began to take a dramatic turn when her mother passed away on October 22, 1912 in Washington, D.C. Nineteen months later, her father died on May 9 in Santa Barbara, California leaving Marjorie the Postum Cereal Company and $20 million.[33] Before dying, C.W. had instilled a lasting legacy in his daughter, "Never let money possess you, never worship it. Do good with it, make it work for you, keep it busy."[34]

In 1915, the Closes moved into The Burden, a mansion in New York City at 2 East 92nd Street, which they purchased the following year. Marjorie preferred the bustling excitement the city provided to the more subdued life in Greenwich. In Manhattan, she began taking art history classes at the Metropolitan Museum of Art, attending concerts at Carnegie Hall, and balls at the Waldorf Astoria Hotel.[35] She and Ed became a part of café society, which was more inclusive than the Four Hundred, so called because only four hundred of the most elite social set could fit into Mrs. William Astor's ballroom. Fashionable clothes were a must for Marjorie's exciting new lifestyle, which included attending Broadway openings. New York was the center of entertainment mixing celebrities and high society on the "Great White Way," as Broadway was known then. During this time, the Closes became friends with Florenz Ziegfeld and his wife, actress Billie Burke.[36] Flo, as he was called, was one of the most influential producers in the history of the Broadway musical. "Flo was producing the [Ziegfeld] Follies at that time," Marjorie said. The *Ziegfeld Follies* (1907–31) were lavish revues filled with glamorous chorus girls wearing spectacular costumes on extravagant sets. "The openings to those Follies were something, it was more than a Hollywood premiere. We always had the best seats for our group because of Flo's friendship. He was a fascinating person," she added.[37]

44
Detail of fig. 45

45
Evening dress
Tan silk velvet, tan lace, green silk organza, rolled silk velvet fringe, clear rhinestones
American, ca. 1912
48.32
This late Edwardian, high-waisted sheath gown illustrates the elegance of women's clothing from the period.

At that time, leading ladies supplied their own costumes for stage performances and Billie had many of hers made by the influential British designer Lucile, aka Lady Duff Gordon. Lucile, a survivor of the *Titanic*, was known internationally for her ultra-feminine, light-as-air, pastel tea dresses, evening gowns, and lingerie embellished with embroideries, buttons, bows, intricately made cloth blossoms, and delicate lace collars. Lucile is credited with holding the first "mannequin parades," or fashion shows. She would invite elite guests, serve a quintessential British afternoon tea, and have models, whom she personally trained, elegantly stroll to the sounds of a string quartet. Along with her strong following among American actresses and socialites, as well as English aristocracy, Lucile also created many costumes for the *Ziegfeld Follies* during World War I.

Billie introduced Marjorie to Lucile, who became one of her favorite fashion designers. Billie also recommended Madame Bob, of Bob, Inc., N.Y., who made Billie's custom shoes for the stage as well as for other luminaries such as noted ballroom dancer Irene Castle. Marjorie custom ordered shoes from Bob, Inc., N.Y. from 1916 through 1971, when the company closed. In fact, when Marjorie died, she left seventy-two pairs of Bob, Inc., N.Y. shoes custom made in size 6½ with a heel height of 2¾ inches. Billie, who later went on to play Glinda the Good Witch of The North in *The Wizard of Oz*, also taught Marjorie how to apply false eyelashes and rouge.[38]

The Closes were spending more time in Manhattan and only going to Greenwich on weekends, holidays, and during the summer.[39] Marjorie was furnishing their city home with fine Louis XVI furniture, Aubusson rugs, Beauvais tapestries, and Sèvres porcelain, despite objections from Ed who found this ostentatious.[40]

During this time, Marjorie was growing more interested in the Women's Suffrage movement, more involved in the Postum Cereal Company, and more independent. The political climate was growing ever darker as World War I was continuing to rage across Europe. The United States entered the war on April 6, 1917.[41] In May, a fire broke out at The Boulders causing severe damage. Marjorie and Ed returned from a dance at the country club to find firefighters tossing trunks of clothes, china, European paintings, and other treasures across the lawn.

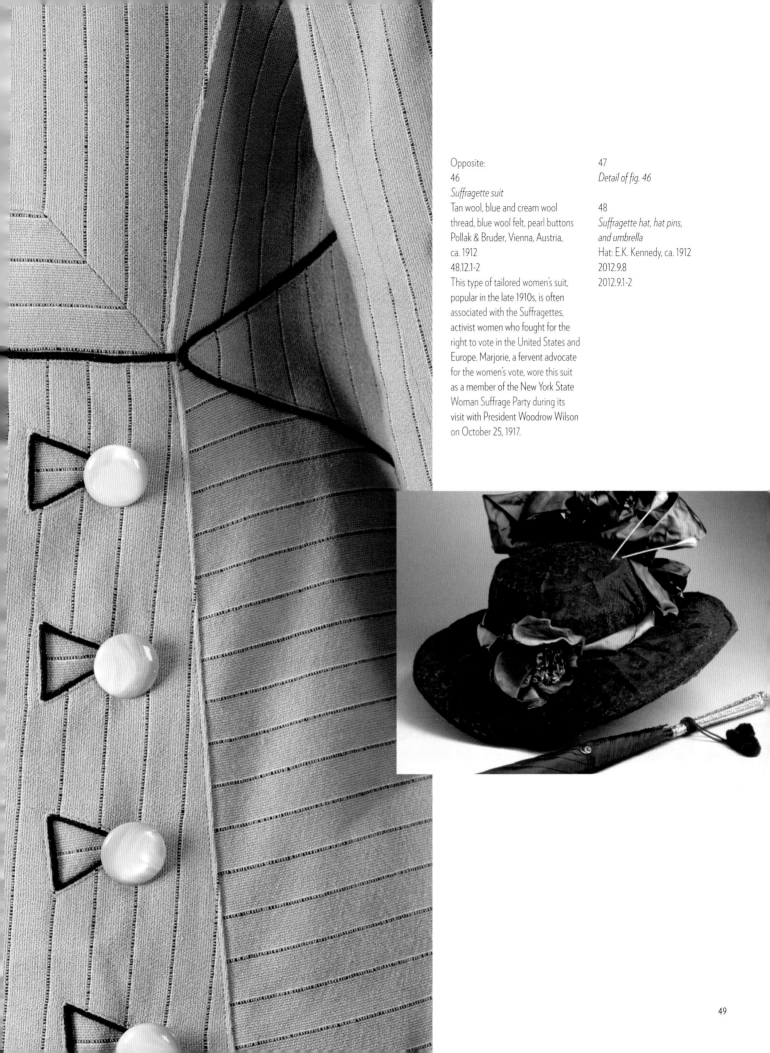

Opposite:
46
Suffragette suit
Tan wool, blue and cream wool thread, blue wool felt, pearl buttons
Pollak & Bruder, Vienna, Austria, ca. 1912
48.12.1-2
This type of tailored women's suit, popular in the late 1910s, is often associated with the Suffragettes, activist women who fought for the right to vote in the United States and Europe. Marjorie, a fervent advocate for the women's vote, wore this suit as a member of the New York State Woman Suffrage Party during its visit with President Woodrow Wilson on October 25, 1917.

47
Detail of fig. 46

48
Suffragette hat, hat pins, and umbrella
Hat: E.K. Kennedy, ca. 1912
2012.9.8
2012.9.1-2

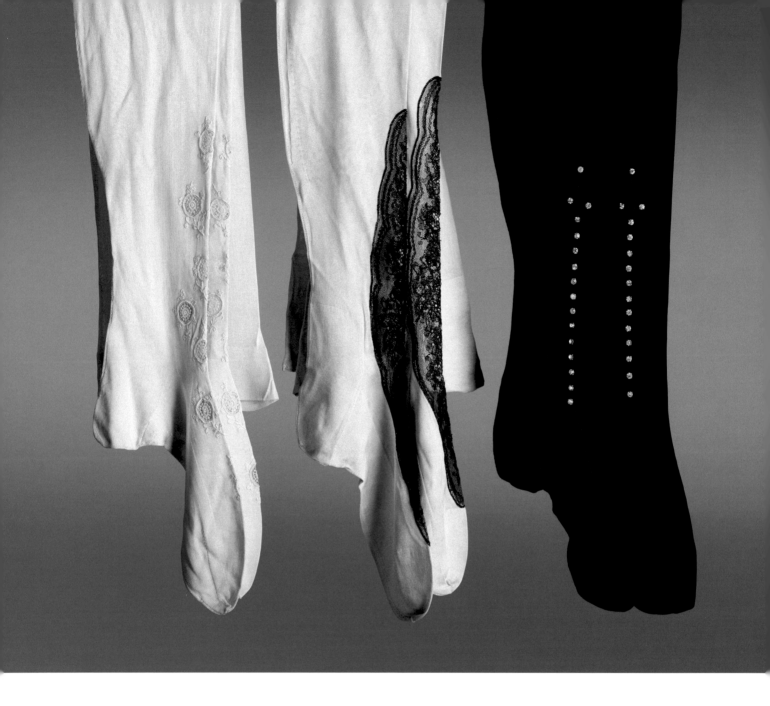

A couple of months later, Edward joined the war effort and set sail for Europe on July 30, 1917. Meanwhile, Marjorie had been knitting, sewing, and rolling bandages for soldiers through the Red Cross, but she wanted to do something more significant. So she contributed to the war effort by financing the Number 8 Base Hospital at Savenay, which grew to be the largest hospital in France with three thousand beds by the end of the war.[42] Marjorie reportedly gave $75,000 for the unit, but the vessel that set sail with the supplies was rammed, sank, and all of the supplies were lost. Undeterred, she funded a second round of supplies eight days later.[43] Marjorie was simultaneously caring for her two growing daughters. Becoming increasingly independent, she joined other committee members of the New York State Woman Suffrage Party and met with President Woodrow Wilson in Washington on October 25.[44] At the same time the war was putting new pressures on the Postum Cereal Company, so Marjorie began taking more of a hands-on approach.[45]

49
Stockings
Makers Unknown, ca. 1915
2014.4.6, 2014.4.8, 2014.4.1, 2014.4.2,
2014.4.4, 2014.4.5
Stockings became an important
fashion accessory as hemlines
rose and more leg was revealed.
Increasingly elaborate ornamentation
was added to the design since there
was more to see. Stockings worn
in the evening were adorned with
rhinestones and lace, while day
stockings were often embroidered
or appliqued.

The year 1918 brought great change. World War I ended and women were on the cusp of winning the right to vote. Marjorie and Ed had been drifting apart for years and by the time he returned from the war, she had made up her mind—she wanted a divorce.[46] The divorce became final in 1919.

That same year, Marjorie commissioned August Benziger, a renowned Swiss artist, to paint a portrait of her and her daughters. He asked her in advance to lay out three or four dresses so he could choose the one he wanted her to wear. The day of the sitting, Marjorie laid out a single gown, a beautiful confection by Lucile. She had made the decision on her own (fig. 50).[47]

Benziger, who created a larger-than-life painting of Marjorie, Eleanor, and Adelaide, seemed mesmerized by this woman, as Marieli Benziger wrote in *August Benziger, Portrait Painter*:

> Though Marjorie Merriweather Post had inherited fame and fortune from her father, Charles William Post of Battle Creek, Michigan, it was the ethereal beauty of his sitter that had captivated the artist's fancy.
>
> August was intrigued. Never before had he met a woman who combined such rare loveliness with such brilliance of mind. Her intuitive business sense held him spellbound. He saw in her the embodiment of all that was best in American womanhood … Here was a personage that would have been the envy of old Europe with all the charm and manners and enthusiasm of the New World.[48]

Benziger was not alone in admiring Marjorie. "On one occasion, when the Prince of Wales saw her in the same elevator, he exclaimed, 'where does this loveliest of all princesses come from? Never have I seen any beauty equal to hers.'"[49]

50
Afternoon dress
White silk lawn, white tulle, pink silk ribbon
Lucile, New York,
ca. 1917
48.41
This tea dress style was popular in the latter half of the 1910s. Marjorie admired this particular trend and had matching dresses made for her daughters as well.

51
Detail of fig. 50

52

*Marjorie Merriweather Post
and Daughters, Eleanor
and Adelaide*
Oil on canvas, 1918
August Benziger
(1867–1955)
51.145
Marjorie selected this
delicate afternoon dress by
Lucile to wear when she and
her daughters, Eleanor and
Adelaide, had their portrait
painted by the renowned
Swiss portrait painter,
August Benziger.

Endnotes

1 Nettie Leitch Major, *C.W. Post, The Hour and The Man; A Biography with Genealogical Supplement* (Washington, D.C.: Judd & Detweiler, 1963), 157.

2 Marjorie Merriweather Post, interview by Nettie Leitch Major, Hot Springs, VA, December 30, 1964, Oral history, Bentley Historical Library, University of Michigan, 18.

3 Ibid.

4 Nancy Rubin, *American Empress: The Life and Times of Marjorie Merriweather Post* (New York: Villard Books, 1995), 21.

5 Post, interview, 1964, 18.

6 Ibid., 12.

7 J. Anderson Black and Madge Garland, *A History of Fashion*, updated and revised by Frances Kennett (New York: William Morrow and Company, 1980), 220.

8 Post, interview, 1964, 55.

9 Major, *C.W. Post*, 85.

10 Post, interview, 1964, 58.

11 Ibid., 58–59.

12 Ibid.

13 "Research Files, Alphabetical Files, 1901–1910," Hillwood Archives.

14 Betty Halbreich (Bergdorf Goodman Personal Shopper), interview by Howard Kurtz, June 16, 2014, Oral history, Hillwood Collection.

15 Black and Garland, *A History of Fashion*, 223.

16 Post, interview, 1964, 17.

17 Black and Garland, *A History of Fashion*, 222.

18 Rubin, *American Empress*, 67.

19 Marjorie Merriweather Post, interview by Nettie Leitch Major, February 1962.

20 Rubin, *American Empress*, 67.

21 Ibid., 67.

22 Ibid.

23 Black and Garland, *A History of Fashion*, 221.

24 Rubin, *American Empress*, 69.

25 Ibid., 70.

26 Post, interview, 1962.

27 William Wright, *Heiress: The Rich Life of Marjorie Merriweather Post* (Washington, D.C.: New Republic Books, 1978), 55.

28 Estella M. Chung, *Living Artfully: At Home with Marjorie Merriweather Post* (Washington, D.C.: Hillwood Museum and Gardens Foundation; London: D Giles Limited, 2013), 13.

29 Ibid.

30 Wright, *Heiress*, 65.

31 Charlotte Seeling, *Fashion: The Century of the Designer, 1900–1999* (Cologne: Könemann, 2000), 20.

32 Black and Garland, *A History of Fashion*, 226.

33 Wright, *Heiress*, 63.

34 Major, *C.W. Post*, 204.

35 Rubin, *American Empress*, 96.

36 Dina Merrill, interview by Howard Kurtz, June 6, 2006, Oral history, Hillwood Collection.

37 Post, interview, 1964, 39.

38 Merrill, interview, 2006.

39 Rubin, *American Empress*, 96.

40 Ibid., 99.

41 Ibid., 97.

42 Ibid., 101.

43 Ibid., 100–101.

44 Ibid., 100.

45 Ibid., 109–10.

46 Ibid., 105.

47 Merrill, interview, 2006.

48 Marieli Benziger, with the assistance of Rita Benziger, *August Benziger, Portrait Painter* (Glendale, CA: The Arthur H. Clark Company, 1958), 422.

49 Ibid.

CHAPTER 2

GLAMOROUS PARTIES AND ALL THAT JAZZ

1920–1934

53
Wedding dress
Lilac gauze organza, light blue silk,
light blue lace
Lucile, New York City, 1920
48.40.1
The wedding dress for Marjorie's
marriage to E.F. Hutton, now
faded, was originally a lilac organza,
decorated with blue fabric flowers,
leaves, and lace bands.

Opposite:
54
Marjorie with her daughters,
Adelaide (left) and Eleanor (right)
Location Unknown, 1920
Marjorie and her daughters wore
matching gowns attributed to Lucile
for Marjorie's wedding to E.F. Hutton.

Previous page:
Marjorie Merriweather Close Hutton
posing for a studio photograph
ca. 1928
Photograph: S'Ora Paris

The fifteen years that followed the end of World War I brought tremendous change in women's fashions. As a euphoric mood swept the nation during what began as an era of prosperity, Marjorie embraced the new styles in clothing, accessories, hair, and makeup. She captured the spirit of Palm Beach, a winter playground for the elite, where she established a strong presence:

> To understand the grand and extravagant behavior in Palm Beach in the '20s, one must realize that World War I was over, the world was "safe for democracy," and prosperity was rampant in the days of low taxes. The average American was doing very well and was fairly secure. Money flowed freely into circulation; that is as it should be, it gives somebody else a chance at it.[1]

With the Jazz Age about to dawn, Marjorie was poised to change with the times. At a houseboat party in Palm Beach in 1919, she encountered Edward Francis Hutton. The two had met a few years earlier at a soirée on Long Island. At this chance meeting Marjorie, now a divorcée, was surprised to learn that the debonair, blond, blue-eyed, and charismatic

owner of his own successful brokerage firm had become a widower.[2] Before long, Marjorie and Ned, as she called him, fell madly in love. The couple married on July 7, 1920 in a quiet ceremony in Marjorie's mansion in Manhattan's "silk-stocking district," the fashionable Upper East Side. The bride chose a simpler design for her second marriage, a romantic, short-sleeve, tea-length lilac and white organza dress trimmed with pale blue fabric flowers, delicate lace, and ribbon (fig. 53). It was designed by Lucile, who earlier in her career had counted Irene Castle, Sarah Bernhardt, film stars, and royalty among her clients.[3] Lucile sold her business in 1918 and was now designing primarily for private clients such as Marjorie, with whom she continued to share a professional relationship. Marjorie's daughters Adelaide and Eleanor, who acted as her bridesmaids, wore lovely designs attributed to Lucile as well. Their dresses featured a playful motif of two intertwining circles or "wedding rings."

The Huttons' union seemed a match made in heaven. Marjorie and Ned each had roots in the Midwest. Ned, reared in Ohio, worked his way up to partner at his uncle's brokerage firm in Cincinnati by age twenty and eventually opened his own firm, the E.F. Hutton Company. Marjorie maintained strong connections to Michigan because the Postum Cereal Company was still based there. By the time they wed,

55
Evening dress
Tan silk velvet, cream tulle, faux
pearls, clear rhinestones
Maker Unknown, French, ca. 1920
48.43
This dress, with its square neckline,
draped velvet skirt and faux
pearl and rhinestone butterfly
embellishments, has a style,
construction, and ornamentation
that suggests French manufacture.

56
Detail of fig. 55

57
Detail of fig. 55

Marjorie at thirty-three and Ned at forty-five,[5] each was already fabulously wealthy. The stage was set for the Huttons to take the world by storm.

The Huttons roared into the twenties, acquiring or building one glamorous home after another. Marjorie already owned The Burden mansion in New York City that she and Ned later razed to allow for a high rise to take its place. They kept the three top floors, which they transformed into a luxurious fifty four-room apartment. The couple built the original Hillwood, an English Jacobean-style country estate on 176 acres along the Gold Coast of Long Island soon after they married.[7] In 1921, they purchased a 207-acre camp surrounded by water in the Adirondacks and named it Hutridge.[8]

They also built Hogarcito, a country cottage in Palm Beach. Marjorie's wardrobe expanded considerably for the various venues and activities, as she moved from one great estate to another. She planned her traveling so she would rarely be in a climate where the temperature was below 72 degrees. Marjorie embraced the new freedom in fashion wholeheartedly and often ordered dresses custom made in different colors and styles, purchasing accessories such as silk stockings and shoes by the half dozen so she would have plenty at her various homes.

The Great War had significantly altered the socially acceptable responsibilities of women. After the war, many women who had joined the workforce during the war chose to continue working as nurses, teachers, clerks, and in manufacturing positions. The newly acquired right to vote gave women more independence, as they found new ways to express their freedom. A new glamour filled the air. Hemlines rose, waistlines dropped, dresses loosened. Locks got bobbed and women began shedding gloves, showing more skin, using makeup, painting fingernails, and wearing jewelry in innovative ways. Opulence ruled. As F. Scott Fitzgerald wrote in *The Great Gatsby*, the early 1920s were a time when "the parties were bigger, the pace was faster, the buildings were higher."

In terms of fashion during the twenties, bold, bright, and saturated colors appeared alongside pale pastels and warm neutrals. Geometrical lines and shapes began to replace floral motifs. Silk velvets, and lamés—first proposed by Callot Soeurs—emerged as popular fabrics for evening wear, while wools, crêpes, cottons, and the novelty jerseys introduced by Chanel were favored for morning, afternoon, and sporting events. The classically influenced dresses of the 1910s evolved into silhouettes that hung farther away from the body and offered more movement, comfort, and ease with pleats, gathers, or slits and shorter hemlines than any other women's fashions in history. Non-restricting chemises were just right for dancing the Charleston. Art Deco influenced clothing design with hard-edged geometric shapes and patterns of concentric circles, parallel lines, step patterns, sunbursts, and stylized florals, many of which made bold fashion statements. Marjorie enjoyed the dramatic changes in fashion and spread her sartorial wings.

58
Negligée robe
Cream silk organza, tulle, silk satin
Maker Unknown, American, ca. 1920
48.62
This negligée robe must have
formed part of Marjorie's trousseau
for her marriage to E.F. Hutton.
It is embroidered with stylized fern
patterns, mirroring the innovative
floral motifs from the 1920s.

59
Tiffany fan
Attributed to Tiffany & Co.,
New York City, ca. 1910
2014.2.12
This fan is masterfully crafted from
ivory inlaid with silver, delicate silver
sequins, and cream silk.

60
*Silk and rhinestone shoes and
bandeau accessories,* ca. 1920
Shoes: J & J Slater, New York City
49.93.1-2
Bandeau: Maker Unknown
2012.9.49
The most fashionable women of
the 1920s wore bandeaus, and on
special occasions adorned heels
and colorful ostrich feather fans
as accessories for evening parties
or soirées at the theater.

61

Afternoon dress
Blue grey silk velvet, blue grey
silk crêpe du chine, peach silk
charmeuse, red orange brocade with
gold metallic thread
Thurn, New York City, ca.1923
48.49.1-2
The end of World War I saw a rise
in the popularity of avant-garde
fashions inspired by the bright colors
and styles of the Ballets Russes.
This afternoon dress suggests
those influences and illustrates the
inspiration of Chinese floral motifs.

62
Detail of fig. 61

While enjoying life to the fullest, Marjorie also cultivated her ingrained sense of philanthropy and her natural disposition to help others. During the winter of 1920–21, the Huttons and friends helped establish a benefit to raise money for a hospital to be built in West Palm Beach. They enlisted Florenz Ziegfeld, one of their closest friends, to lend them costumes and stage sets from his Broadway productions and even a few professionals who performed with the amateurs, young wealthy couples who were wintering in Palm Beach. Marjorie wore a sparkling Ziegfeld costume and the production, a huge hit, raised $110,000 toward the establishment of what was to become the Good Samaritan Hospital of West Palm Beach. Years later, Marjorie recalled:

> I did have a funny experience that night, just as I went on the stage, Francis Brook, one of the stage managers, he came up to me and said, "Marjorie, you don't know how to put your lipstick on, do you?" I replied that I used lipstick and it was all right. He promptly told me that it had to curve, so [he] fixed it and shoved me onstage.[9]

63
Marjorie Merriweather Post Hutton
New York City, 1921
For this portrait sitting, Marjorie wore a gown similar to fig. 64. She often ordered multiple sets of the same style. The most visible difference between the two dresses is the color of the netting at the sleeves and waist.

64
Evening dress
Black silk, black tulle, black and gold brocade
Madeleine & Madeleine, Paris, 1921
48.42
This evening dress features a bifurcated or divided skirt, inspired by the harem pants created for dancers in the Ballets Russes. Parisian couturiers soon thereafter launched this style as a popular fashion for women.

65
Madeleine & Madeleine designer rendering
Photograph: Jean S. and Frederic A. Sharf Collection
A designer sketch from the house of Madeleine & Madeleine illustrates the "Dragon" model, introduced in the summer collection of 1922. The dress is similar to that in fig. 64.

In 1922, the Huttons had an elegant private railway car, originally christened the *Hussar*, built to transport themselves and their guests from New York to Palm Beach and the Adirondacks, depending on the season.[10] In 1923, Ned became chairman of the Postum Cereal Company, which he and Marjorie expanded through acquisitions of other companies. Ned, an avid yachtsman, purchased a luxurious new yacht, the *Hussar IV*, a three-masted schooner that featured five beautifully appointed staterooms, each with a private bathroom.[11] *The Telegraph*, on August 26, 1923, described it thus:

> Hutton's new steam yacht is a humdinger, the finest in the world. He already had another. Wonderful, aren't we, we American millionaires? And then to be pretty besides, for Mrs. Hutton is extraordinarily pretty and nice. Well, it's just too much luck all lumped up in one place.[12]

Indeed, the Huttons lived life to the fullest, regularly attending black tie dinners, dances, fancy dress balls, theater and opera openings, playing golf, and going off to the races in Palm Beach and/or New York. In 1923, the couple was blessed with a daughter Nedenia, who adopted the stage name of Dina Merrill when she grew up and became an actress.

Elaborate costume balls were a favorite form of entertainment in high society circles during the twenties, one of the most opulent and exuberant decades of American history. When the Huttons attended fancy dress balls, such as the Everglades Ball in Palm Beach and the Beaux Arts Ball in Manhattan, Marjorie dressed with gusto. In addition to having her costumes custom made by top designers or professional costume companies, she accented them with wigs, makeup, feathered fans, and exquisite jewels often commissioned from Cartier. Everything about these fancy dress balls was spectacular, from the settings to the splendid costumes. Sometimes in Palm Beach, for example, they involved outdoor dancing under the stars. One element that distinguished these fêtes and added an air of authenticity were the *tableaux vivants,* created when guests would pose frozen in front of painted backdrops that reflected the theme of the evening, so society photographers could take their pictures.

Marie Antoinette was one of Marjorie's favorite historical characters and over the years she had several costumes made so she could play the French queen at various fancy dress balls. A beautiful hand-tinted photograph by Frank E. Geisler in 1923 shows Marjorie dressed as Marie Antoinette gracefully descending the steps of Hogarcito (see fig. 69). Marjorie preserved one extravagant Marie Antoinette costume by Madame Frances (Frances Spingold), a designer and custom dressmaker with an atelier on West 56th Street in Manhattan who also designed for the *Ziegfeld Follies*. Marjorie even saved the feathered headdress and exquisite leather shoes that accompanied the ensemble (see fig. 73). Marjorie was so exacting in her outfits for costume balls that she requested the construction of authentic undergarments for the appropriate silhouette of the gown.

66
Marjorie with her young daughter, Nedenia
New York City, 1924
For this photograph Marjorie wore a flowing dressing gown, a symbol of domesticity and motherhood and a garment that would only have been worn in the privacy of the home.

67
Evening dress
Cream silk velvet, light blue
silk organza, blue glass beads,
rhinestones
Madame Frances, New York City,
ca. 1925
48.44.1-2
In the mid-1920s the prototypical jazz
age fashion of drop-waisted, highly
adorned, loose fitting, tubular dresses
emerged. This dress in ivory and deep
blue velvet trimmed with sparkling
rhinestones and beads illustrates all
these new fashion trends.

68
Purse and fan
Purse: Madame Frances, New York
City, ca. 1925
49.6
Fan: Maker Unknown
2014.3.18
These accessories match the dress
in fig. 67.

On March 9, 1924, when Marjorie dressed as the queen, *The New York Tribune* wrote: : "First Prize Winner at the Everglades Ball, Mrs. Edward F. Hutton takes the honors with a Louis XVI costume." Years later, fashion photographer Cecil Beaton told *Vogue*, "Mrs. Hutton is unsurpassable as Marie Antoinette."[13]

By the mid-1920s, with the help of Viennese architect and set designer Joseph Urban, who had designed backdrops for the *Ziegfeld Follies* and the Metropolitan Opera, the Huttons began construction on an extravagant Hispano-Moresque estate they called Mar-a-Lago in Palm Beach. The 125-room mansion, situated on 17.7 acres with 450 feet of beachfront along the Atlantic Ocean on one side and Lake Worth on the other, provided a spectacular venue for the Huttons to host lavish dinners and big costume balls. In 1926, Marjorie's Starry Night flapper-style costume, which is attributed to Lucile, with its silk crêpe, silk fringe, rhinestones, and sequins evoked the *Ziegfeld Follies* (see figs. 74, 75).

69
Hand-Colored Photograph of Marjorie as Marie Antoinette
Palm Beach, Florida, 1923
Photograph: Frank E. Geisler
Marjorie stepped out of Hogarcito, the Hutton's first home in Palm Beach, ready to attend a fancy dress costume ball dressed as Marie Antoinette.

70
Marie Antoinette costume
Tan and copper silk taffeta, tan and copper silk charmeuse, cream lace, multicolored grosgrain ribbon
Attributed to Madame Frances, American, 1923
48.136.1-3
Spurred on by her fervent interest in French history and the arts of Marie Antoinette's period, Marjorie had multiple costumes made to emulate the French queen at fancy dress balls.

71
Detail of fig. 70

72
Marie Antoinette folding leaf fan
Maker Unknown, late 19th or early 20th century
49.26
This fan consists of hand-painted silk, lace leaf, and mother-of-pearl sticks with metal inlays.

73
Marjorie dressed as Marie Antoinette
for the Beaux Arts Ball
New York City, 1927
Photograph: Gabor Eder
Marjorie posed as Marie Antoinette
in the French drawing room of her
New York home.

74
"Starry Night" costume
Black silk crêpe, rhinestones, blue
and silver sequins
Attributed to Lucile, New York City,
1926
48.138.1-5
Marjorie's "Starry Night" costume
has a direct connection to the
Ziegfeld Follies, and was perhaps
one of the actual costumes
created by the designer Lucile
for a Ziegfeld production.

75
Marjorie dressed in her "Starry Night"
costume for the Everglades Ball
Palm Beach, Florida, 1926
Marjorie wore this highly stylized
version of a *Ziegfeld Follies* costume
at the Everglades Ball. She may have
obtained this costume through her
close friends from the Broadway
stage, producer Florenz Ziegfeld and
his wife, actress Billie Burke.

Opposite:
76
Marjorie as Juliet at the Everglades
Ball, Palm Beach
Palm Beach, Florida, 1929
Marjorie's Renaissance-style Juliet
costume is made of salmon-colored
brocade trimmed in metallic copper
and gold and decorated with
elaborate costume jewels, including
large green pastes and teardrop
faux pearls. Juxtaposed with the
large faux rhinestones, Marjorie
wore a stunning Cartier Indian-style
ensemble consisting of a pendant
brooch suspended from a necklace,
both featuring large emerald beads
mounted in platinum and diamonds.

77
*Marjorie and Nedenia
dressed for Adelaide's wedding*
New York City, 1927

78
Day dress
Caramel velvet, brown silk organza,
cream silk charmeuse, metallic
threads
Bergdorf Goodman, New York City,
1927
48.57.1-2
Worn as a mother-of-the-bride dress
when eldest daughter Adelaide
married Thomas Welles Durant
in the winter of 1927, this caramel
colored velvet dress was specially
ordered at Bergdorf Goodman.

79
Detail of fig. 78

80
Cloche to accompany day dress
Bergdorf Goodman, 1927
48.57.3
81
Shoes to accompany day dress
J & J Slater, New York City 1927
49.98.1-2
These accessories match the dress
in fig. 78.

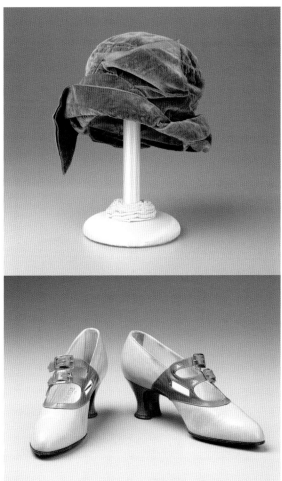

82
Marjorie Merriweather Post Hutton in her court presentation attire
Oil on canvas, 1931
Giulio de Blaas (1888–1934)
Italy
51.149
Two years after Marjorie was presented at the Court of St. James's she had her portrait painted wearing the same ensemble.

Opposite:
83
Court presentation gown
Green silk organza, cream silk organza
Attributed to Callot Soeurs, Paris, 1929
48.64.1-2
Marjorie's presentation gown to the British Royal Court of St. James's adhered to the specific rules of court etiquette. These instructions included specific colors of the gown, the length of her train, and the style of her veil.

84
Detail of fig. 83

Fluttering Skirts Animate
Ritz Holiday Dance

85
Women's Wear Daily article with
sketch of Marjorie and daughter,
Eleanor
New York City, 1927
In December of 1927, *Women's Wear
Daily* featured sketches of some of
the most fashionable attendees to
the winter debutante balls. Both
Marjorie and her daughter, Eleanor,
were featured.

In late fall 1926, Marjorie and Ned hosted Adelaide's debut at The Ritz-Carlton Hotel in Manhattan. It was important to Marjorie that her daughters be presented to society, since she had never had a debut.[14] Traditionally, when a family presented their daughter to society it was to announce her eligibility for marriage. In Adelaide's case, however, she announced that she was engaged the morning after her debut. Marjorie planned every exquisite detail of her first child's wedding, held on January 19, 1927. Adelaide wore a lovely satin gown with a four-foot-long court train embellished with silk net and orange blossoms.[15] The *pièce de résistance* of her bridal ensemble was her historical veil, which Marjorie had acquired in 1925. It had been created for the wedding of Princess Stephanie of Belgium to Crown Prince Rudolph of Austria–Hungary. Marjorie had purchased it directly from their daughter, Elisabeth. She later donated the lace to the Smithsonian. Rave reports followed the celebration, including this one from the *New York American*, which said, "Not since the era of lavish Vanderbilt weddings has metropolitan society gazed upon such a picturesque scene."

86
Evening ensemble
Sheer green silk chiffon, cream silk charmeuse, fox fur, clear rhinestones, faux pearls, bugle beads
Madame Frances, New York City, 1927
48.50.1-3
Marjorie wore this custom design to her second daughter, Eleanor's debut at The Ritz-Carlton Hotel in December 1927. The ensemble, comprised of a dress and cape, nods to the spirit of the Christmas holidays with its decorative mistletoe motifs.

87
Detail of fig. 86

Eleanor, Marjorie's second daughter, made her debut to New York society at Christmas that year. Joseph Urban theatrically designed the Grand Ballroom of The Ritz-Carlton, New York with silver gauze backlit with spotlights and a profusion of flowers.[16] In May of 1928, Eleanor was also presented at the Court of St. James's in London, where she wore a beautiful custom-made turquoise blue gown designed by Madame Frances.

Fulfilling a lifelong dream, in June of 1929, Marjorie herself was presented in London at the Court of St. James's to King George V and Queen Mary. Her presentation represented a momentous social accomplishment, especially given the fact that few divorced women were permitted to be presented in the late 1920s. Marjorie, 42, received a letter prior to her visit that intricately detailed the ceremonial protocol to be followed in regard to the length of the train, the fan, bouquet allowances, and the appropriate headdress. Marjorie wore a lovely seafoam silk organza sleeveless gown with a dropped waist, a raised hemline in the front, and a train attached at shoulder height that was easily detachable to accommodate dancing after the court ceremonies had concluded. Exquisite, feathery beading graced the hips in this gown possibly designed by the famed Callot Soeurs, who had started the House of Callot in 1895 and were among the leading designers in Paris during the 1920s. Callot Soeurs catered to actresses and exclusive American and European clients.[17] Marjorie wore the customary veil with three white ostrich feathers, which signaled she was married. Single women wore two feathers. Marjorie accented her beautiful ensemble with stunning Cartier jewels, including pendant earrings with pear-shaped diamonds that had once belonged to Marie Antoinette as well as a 21 carat Colombian emerald, said to have belonged to the ill-fated Maximilian, Emperor of Mexico, which Cartier mounted for her. Marjorie later commissioned Giulio de Blaas to paint a full-length oil portrait of her in her exquisite court attire (see figs. 82–84).

Throughout the 1920s, Eva Stotesbury, known to Palm Beachers as the "grande dame of the winter set," had taken Marjorie under her wing.[18] She was "an aunt to me and a dear friend," Marjorie later said of the woman who had groomed her to become her social successor.[19] Marjorie recalled one celebration in particular:

> One party I well remember was Mrs. Stotesbury's swimming party at the Bath & Tennis [Club]; … Irene Castle … won the prize for the prettiest costume, and I won the prize for the funniest … I wore a gunny sack with kitchen utensils hanging all over me. It was great fun.[20]

Marjorie's striking Juliet costume, which she wore to the Palm Beach Everglades Ball in 1929, was a Renaissance-style gown made by the costume company Schneider-Anderson that featured real gold and copper threads, paste jewels, and faux pearl embellishments. But Marjorie created the *crème de la crème* of costumes when she added her breathtaking Cartier Mughal emerald and diamond *sautoir* (long necklace) and her emerald and diamond shoulder clip brooch in a platinum setting, which she wore as a pendant. She won first place in the Ball's costume competition (see fig. 76).

The Native American costume Marjorie wore for the 1929 Whoopee Ball in Palm Beach was another entrance maker with its beaded white tunic dress, turquoise velvet cape lined with marabou feathers and beaded and feathered headdress, all made by the Eaves Costume

88
Marjorie with her three daughters:
Adelaide (left), Nedenia (center),
and Eleanor (right)
New York City, ca. 1927
Photograph: Ira Hill Studio
Marjorie posed with her three
daughters wearing a velvet dress
with geometrical art deco motifs.

89
Evening dress
Red silk velvet, cream silk crêpe,
red glass beads, metallic threads,
rhinestones
Thurn, New York City, 1926
48.45
Marjorie wore this gown to her eldest
daughter Adelaide's debut at The
Ritz-Carlton Hotel in the fall of 1926.
Gone were the soft frills, ruffles,
and laces of the previous decades,
replaced by metallic adornments,
strong contrasts, bold shapes,
saturated colors, asymmetry, and rich,
dense fabrics.

90
Detail of fig. 89

91, 92
Evening ensemble
Red silk crêpe, melon silk charmeuse,
organza, lace
Thurn, New York City, ca. 1927
48.60.1-3
With bright, multi-colored,
geometric patches on the skirt and
cape, this evening ensemble is an
excellent example of the avant-garde
influences in fashion during the late
1920s. The abstract patterns are
reminiscent of the work of Kandinsky,
Picasso, and Mondrian.

93
Detail of fig. 91

94
Evening dress
Black silk velvet, black tulle, rhinestones, black silk charmeuse, and nude silk organza
Bergdorf Goodman, New York City, 1929
48.47
This dress has a full skirt and train, an alternative to the more predominant tubular sheath style dress of the 1920s. This French fashion quickly caught on and became popular with chic women. Marjorie's dress features a decorative bow and ties running vertically down the center of the skirt.

95
Detail of fig. 94

96
Ostrich feather fan
Maker Unknown, ca. 1920
2014.3.15
This dramatic black and white ostrich feather fan epitomizes the large feather fans that were so popular in the 1920s.

Company in New York. The Huttons' fascination with Native American cultures extended beyond their clothing for fancy dress balls. They also collected Native American objects, such as baskets, Cheyenne cradles, and Sioux moccasins, for display at Hutridge, their estate in the Adirondacks.[21]

While Marjorie often wore the latest in fashion and was collecting the finest of jewels, she was very content with over-the-counter cosmetics purchased from department stores. She began wearing Tangee lipstick in an orange/pink shade and Revlon Liquid Nail Enamel in "Red," which she applied herself. And she used castor oil on her skin rather than expensive moisturizer.[22] She continued using these products throughout the rest of her life.

Marjorie was adamant about protecting her skin from the sun, at a time when suntans were becoming popular. She once told a fair-skinned friend, "Stay out of the sun. People who go in it look like alligators later in life." And she practiced what she preached, going to extremes to cover herself on those rare occasions that she went to the beach, to the dismay of her daughters. "Mom had these real long-sleeve bathing suits she had concocted for herself with bare midriffs and a little skirt. Then she'd wear her gloves and a hat and her bathing cap and dark glasses," recalled Nedenia.[23] Avoiding UVA and UVB rays paid off. As one of Marjorie's guests said years later, "She comes into a room and everyone else looks exhausted."[24]

While life was running fairly smoothly for Marjorie and Ned, all was not perfect. Once when Marjorie learned that Ned had lost $50,000 when gambling one night in Palm Beach, she told him that if he ever did that again, she would go out and "spend double of whatever amount you lose."[25] When he lost another $50,000 gambling, Marjorie purchased a lovely strand of pearls for more than $100,000, and had the bill sent to Ned.

Marjorie was also getting more involved in Postum business throughout the 1920s and often gave Ned suggestions. After tasting frozen goose in the early 1920s, she had urged Ned to buy Clarence Birdseye's company, convinced that the workloads for American housewives would be reduced considerably. She did not relent until he purchased it in June 1929. Her tenacity demonstrated her business prowess and understanding of women's needs. The acquisition proved to be an excellent investment for her company.

97
Marjorie at the Saratoga races
New York, 1930
Photograph by Rotofoto
Dressed for the horse races at
Saratoga, Marjorie wore a bold,
asymmetrical, grey crêpe dress by
Jay Thorpe.

Opposite:
98
Day dress
Grey waffle crêpe, cream satin
Jay Thorpe, New York City, 1930
48.88
Marjorie wore this day dress
to the Saratoga Racetrack in
New York in 1930 (fig. 97). The
outfit encapsulates the dramatic
transformations in fashion after the
Roaring Twenties and the advent
of the Great Depression. Far more
practical, stripped of adornment,
and of modern design, this dress
announces the more austere 1930s.

99
Detail of fig. 98

100
Parrot hat to accompany day dress
Jay Thorpe, New York City, 1930
2012.9.45
Marjorie wore this exotic hat adorned
with bright green parrot feathers to
the races in Saratoga in 1930.

When Black Tuesday hit on October 29, 1929, it brought the end of an era. As Marjorie remembered, "Then came the Depression and a reality that changed the status of most of the population."[26] Marjorie felt compelled to act. She stored her jewels in the bank and used the money she saved from insurance to open the Marjorie Post Hutton Canteen, a soup kitchen originally intended to feed women and children that later expanded to feed older and infirm men who didn't have the strength to make the trip downtown to the Edward F. Hutton Food Station for Men, which Ned had established. The Hutton canteens operated from 1929 to 1935, providing meals and sustenance to countless people.

Marjorie devoted significant time to organizing fundraisers for various charities, including an anti-crime campaign, and she was earning a reputation for her generous philanthropy. Incoming First Lady Eleanor Roosevelt awarded Marjorie the Cross of Honor from the United States Flag Association on December 12, 1932 at the White House for her charitable work.[27] She was named as one of the "10 Women over 30 as Most Charming in the Nation," by the National Association for American Speech, because of her public service.[28]

101
Marjorie seated at the beach with a friend
Palm Beach, Florida, 1920
Always very protective of her skin, she covered herself completely at the beach, even wearing gloves.

Meanwhile, talking pictures had become the rage by the late 1920s and at the height of the Golden Age of Hollywood in the '30s, fashion and film became intricately intertwined. The glamorous attire of legendary movie stars, such as Greta Garbo, Bette Davis, Jean Harlow, and Katharine Hepburn, influenced everyone from Seventh Avenue garment houses and design staffs at department stores to women in high society.[29] The era ushered in a new focus on style as Hollywood designers, including Gilbert Adrian, Walter Plunkett, Travis Banton, and Edith Head, created some of the most alluring, evocative, and flattering fashions of all time. Clothing, designed closer to the body than in the twenties, skimmed women's figures in sensuous fabrics such as satins, chiffons, lamés, and silk charmeuses, all played against a backdrop of spectacular sets. Not only did designers create elaborate costumes with changes for almost every scene, it was common practice to insert a fashion show within a film. During the Great Depression, movies captivated glamour-starved audiences inspiring them to dream of a world filled with bubble baths, baubles, and

102
Marjorie on the Hussar
ca. 1930
Always a picture of style and grace,
Marjorie posed in a skirt, belted
blouse, and jacket aboard her
luxurious yacht.

103
Hussar V shoes
Bob Shoes, Inc., New York City, 1931
49.28.1-2
Marjorie had these hard sole boudoir
slippers custom made by Bob, Inc.
for use on her yacht, the *Hussar V,*
which she renamed the *Sea Cloud*
in 1935.

dazzling beaded evening gowns. Marjorie integrated the sensuous looks of Hollywood into her wardrobe and even took things one step further. She ordered her custom-made gowns with the waistband one-inch higher than her natural waist to help create the illusion that her legs looked longer. By this point, she was very self-assured and knew the image she wanted to project.

While others were getting lost in the fantasy of Hollywood, the Huttons and their youngest daughter, Nedenia, had another way to escape the harsh realities of the Depression. The *Hussar V,* their new ultra-luxurious yacht, christened in the *Guinness Book of Records* as the world's largest privately owned sailing yacht, complete with a crew of seventy-two, a cinema, and even a team of doctors, was launched in 1931.[30] The Huttons traveled at least six months a year from 1932 to 1934 aboard their handsome new windjammer, having adventures in the Galápagos Islands, Tahiti, Hawaii, Alaska, and across the Atlantic to the Loire River in France.[31]

104
Marjorie posing for Frank O. Salisbury painting
New York City, ca. 1934
Marjorie gave painter Frank Salisbury this photo to use as a reference while working on her portrait in 1934.

Opposite:
105
Evening dress
Cream silk crêpe, cream organza
Maker Unknown, American, ca. 1933
48.75
An excellent study of 1930s fashions, this evening gown displays a smooth, sleek, form-fitting bias cut, with an asymmetrical design. In stark contrast to the fashions from the previous decade, superfluous adornment has been stripped from the dress to make the body the focal point.

106
*Portrait of Marjorie Merriweather
Post Hutton*
Oil on canvas 1934
Frank O. Salisbury (1874–1962)
New York City
51.140
Marjorie wore a stunning silk satin
ivory bias-cut dress with a red silk
velvet drape trimmed in white fox fur
for this portrait. She complemented
her glamorous attire with a ruby
and diamond clip securing the
gown's back and Cartier bracelets of
platinum, diamonds, and rubies.

Nedenia remembers her mother always being impeccably dressed. "Mother always wore a corset, even in the tropics," she said. Marjorie also donned sarongs, shorts, or whatever warm-weather fashions were appropriate to the locale.

Despite sailing around the world together to places that seemed like paradise, Marjorie and Ned were actually drifting apart. They had very different views about politics in particular. Marjorie was pro President Franklin D. Roosevelt's policies and Ned was adamantly against them. But even worse, Marjorie would discover that Ned had a wandering eye. To the average onlooker, however, things seemed fine. In fact, Marjorie sat for an oil portrait with the renowned English artist Frank Owen Salisbury wearing a glamorous white, bias-cut, satin, sleeveless dress with a low-cut, V-back fastened by a ruby and diamond brooch and a long two-strand pearl necklace (fig. 106).

After that sitting, Salisbury said of Marjorie, "It is seldom that an artist has a sitter who knows to perfection the gowns and jewels that suit her best, or where in the house the portrait should be hung, and who with tactful grace can pose without cramping the artist's work." He continued, "Her portrait made a decorative picture, with a dress of ivory satin and a rich red velvet cloak. She had a remarkable silver strand in her hair."[32]

Endnotes

1 Marjorie Merriweather Post, as related to Nettie Leitch Major for purposes of a biography and transcribed from tape recordings, Palm Beach, by February 1965, Bentley Historical Library, University of Michigan.

2 Nancy Rubin, *American Empress: The Life and Times of Marjorie Merriweather Post* (New York: Villard Books, 1995), 106–7.

3 Georgina O'Hara Callan, *The Thames & Hudson Dictionary of Fashion and Fashion Designers* (London: Thames & Hudson, 1998), 156.

4 Ibid.

5 Rubin, *American Empress*, 107.

6 Stefano Papi and Alexandra Rhodes, *20th Century Jewelry & The Icons of Style* (London: Thames & Hudson, 2013), 9.

7 Rubin, *American Empress*, 121.

8 Ibid., 123.

9 Marjorie Merriweather Post, as related to Nettie Leitch Major, 5.

10 Michael L. Grace, "Marjorie Merriweather Post's Private Railway Car," http://www.newyorksocialdiary.com/node/136304/print.

11 Rubin, *American Empress*, 137–38.

12 Cynthia's Letter, *The Telegraph*, nationally syndicated column, August 26, 1923; Hillwood Collection Archives.

13 Cecil Beaton, "Suggestions for Fancy Dress," *Vogue*, December 1937.

14 Rubin, *American Empress*, 170.

15 Ibid., 172.

16 Rubin, *American Empress*, 176.

17 Lisa Sanderson, "Callot Soeurs," June 14, 2009, https://Suite.io/lisa-sanderson/1wck233.

18 Rubin, *American Empress*, 112.

19 Marjorie Merriweather Post, as related to Nettie Leitch Major, 3.

20 Ibid.

21 Estella M. Chung, *Living Artfully: At Home with Marjorie Merriweather Post* (Washington, D.C.: Hillwood Museum and Gardens Foundation; London: D Giles Limited, 2013), 57.

22 Nettie Leitch Major, *C.W. Post, The Hour and The Man: A Biography with Genealogical Supplement* (Washington, D.C.: Judd & Detweiler, 1963), 203.

23 Rubin, *American Empress*, 42.

24 *Life*, November 5, 1965, 54.

25 Rubin, *American Empress*, 149.

26 Marjorie Merriweather Post, as related to Nettie Leitch Major.

27 Ibid.

28 Rubin, *American Empress*, 184.

29 Sarah Tomerlin Lee, ed., *American Fashion, The Life and Lines of Adrian, Mainbocher, McCardell, Norell, Trigère* (New York: Quadrangle, 1975), 24.

30 Rubin, *American Empress*, 185.

31 Ibid., 187–88.

32 Frank O. Salisbury, *Portrait and Pageant* (1944), rev. as *Sarum Chase* (London: John Murray, 1953), 108.

A SARTORIAL SUCCESS AT HOME AND ABROAD

1935–1954

107
Marjorie with granddaughter Marwee (left), and daughter Nedenia (center) when she wed Joseph E. Davies
New York City, 1935
The glamour and theatrical influence of Hollywood on contemporary fashion is reflected in this wedding photograph of Marjorie with her attendants.

Previous page:
Marjorie Post Hutton posing for a studio photograph
1932
Photograph: Underwood & Underwood

arjorie looked like she could have stepped right off the silver screen when she wore an ultra-glamorous bridal gown to marry Joseph Davies in an intimate ceremony in her New York apartment on December 15, 1935. The two had met at a dinner party in Palm Beach and discovered they shared many things in common, particularly their mutual support of President Franklin D. Roosevelt's policies. Joe, a prominent international lawyer, was a longtime friend and advisor to the president. Marjorie's form-fitting, long-sleeve, peach velvet gown, which she had custom made at Bergdorf Goodman, featured a dramatic sweeping train trimmed in white fox. Nedenia, her daughter and maid of honor, wore a pale blue satin empire gown with puffed sleeves and a train trimmed in pleated tulle. Marwee Durant, Marjorie's granddaughter and bridesmaid, wore a matching pale blue gown (figs. 107–109).

108
Wedding gown
Peach silk velvet, white fox
Bergdorf Goodman, New York City, 1935
48.80
Evoking the drama and glamour of Hollywood, Marjorie's wedding gown was a form-fitting, peach velvet design with a dramatic train trimmed in white fox.

109
Detail of fig. 108
The Bergdorf Goodman label sewn inside Marjorie's wedding dress.

110
Boudoir gown
Peach silk crêpe, machine yellow
Valenciennes lace
Attributed to Bergdorf Goodman,
1935
48.81.1-2
This two-piece boudoir gown must
have been part of Marjorie's wedding
trousseau for her marriage to Joseph
E. Davies in 1935. Boudoir gowns
were worn in the home.

111
Gown on lingerie board

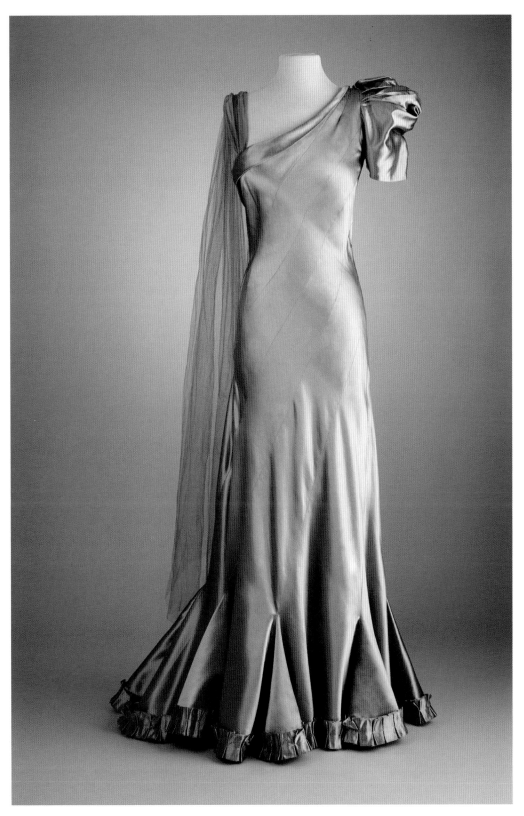

112
Evening dress
Copper cotton-backed satin, copper tulle, copper silk crêpe
Robert Piguet, Paris, ca. 1935
48.76
A mixture of fashion trends from the period, this copper-colored evening dress features asymmetrical sleeves, bias-cut fabrics, and cuffed collar. One of Marjorie's favorite styles, she had the gown made in both copper and ivory.

113
Evening dress (front)
Printed cotton, cream silk charmeuse,
cream organza, cream tulle
Bergdorf Goodman, New York City,
ca. 1935
48.68.1-2
Typical of fashions from the
early 1930s, this dress is made of
diaphanous layers of fabric and a
printed paisley motif. It illustrates
the newest fashion for form-fitting
dresses with broad shoulders, narrow
waists, and trailing trains.

114
Evening dress (back)

115
Detail of fig. 113

116
Evening dress
Silk taffeta
Maker Unknown, American, ca. 1935
48.70
The strong geometric shapes and
abstract graphic patterns displayed
on this dress are reminiscent of the
paintings by Robert Delaunay and
the fabric designs of his wife, Sonia.

117
Detail of fig. 116

118
Evening dress
Grey and white fern pattern silk taffeta, red taffeta
Maker Unknown, American, 1934
48.69
The bold white fern pattern on this grey bias-cut dress reflects the stylized designs of the 1930s. The bow and loose ties at the back of the waist, lined in bright red taffeta, are loosely inspired by the Japanese obi, the sash for traditional Japanese dress.

119
Marjorie in her New York home
1934
Photographed in the entryway of her New York home, Marjorie is wearing the fern patterned dress in fig. 118.

120
Dressing gown
Cream silk crêpe, cream ostrich feathers
The White House, London, ca. 1930
18.82
Marjorie would have worn this ultra-glamorous dressing gown in the morning while taking care of personal tasks in her private rooms.

121
Lounging gown
Black silk crêpe
Toute Prête, Inc., New York City, ca. 1935
48.86
Marjorie would have worn this lounging gown, with its fringed and theatrical bat sleeves, at home.

122
Lounging gown
Blue velvet, metal
Maker Unknown, America, ca. 1940
48.133
This velvet lounging gown, complete with a train, was for an evening at home.

Joe, 58, and Marjorie, 47, spent several months on their honeymoon cruising on her luxurious yacht, formerly the *Hussar V,* which she renamed the *Sea Cloud* after divorcing Ned Hutton earlier in 1935. The newlyweds sailed to Rio de Janeiro, Buenos Aires, and Caracas, among many other exotic ports. "What a year it's been—the heights and the depths. But now we are in the peaceful waters—all my dreams come true," Marjorie wrote in her large, distinctive handwriting in her scrapbook dated 1935–36.[1]

After returning from their honeymoon, Marjorie received a rare distinction when she was elected to the board of directors of the General Foods Corporation on April 8, 1936, the first woman to be chosen in the history of the company. She was actually among the first women to be named to the board of any major American corporation. "Again back into my Daddy's business!" Marjorie wrote in her scrapbook in between newspaper clippings announcing her election.[2]

Marjorie always made a special effort to dress well for her board meetings, recalled Ellen MacNeille Charles, Adelaide's second daughter and Marjorie's granddaughter. "I always have to get dressed up for my boys' meetings," Marjorie, who wore well-tailored suits with feminine blouses, told Ellen. "You know they like a woman to look nice, even if they don't say anything about it," Marjorie explained. Former *Washington Post* reporter Roy Meacham described Marjorie saying, "She kept that steel-trap mind behind a veil of femininity."[3]

In August of 1936, while in the Adirondacks at Topridge, formerly known as Hutridge, Joe received a summons to the White House. President Roosevelt had appointed him U.S. Ambassador to Soviet Russia. Marjorie was surprised by the news, because Moscow was a far cry from the plum assignment to a European capital that she had anticipated. One of her biggest fears was not the remote location of the country, but the sub-zero temperatures of the Russian winters. Years later, Marjorie recalled:

> I had been living in the semi-tropics in the winters for at least thirty years and while I was raised in a country of heavy snows … it had been a long time since I had experienced anything like that.[4]

123
Day dress
Yellow silk with tropical flower motif
Gervais, New York City, ca. 1930
48.71
Most likely a summer day dress, this vibrant day wrap dress displays the 1930s craze for tropical prints. This fad was popularized by Hollywood films and nightclubs such as the Coconut Grove.

124
Evening ensemble
Coral silk velvet, white fox, metallic gold thread
Thurn, New York City, ca. 1935
48.72.1-2
This evening ensemble is made of coral velvet with an empire waist, a bodice with velvet flowers, and short, slightly puffed sleeves. The dress is completed with a matching rectangular drape trimmed with white fox fur.

125
Marjorie at Mar-a-Lago
Palm Beach, Florida, ca. 1930

Marjorie immediately began assembling a wardrobe to protect her from Russia's bitterly cold winters. She ordered new clothes and had others altered. For example, she went to Bergdorf Goodman to have her tweed coats lined with chamois for extra insulation. When asked why she was lining her coat, Marjorie, who needed to be discreet because her husband's ambassadorship had yet to be made public, nonchalantly replied, "I feel a little chill coming on."[5]

Being an ambassador's wife represented a turning point in Marjorie's approach to fashion. Knowing she was about to represent America abroad at her husband's side, she sought out designers and dressmakers working in America to design her clothing. Rosie Renault, who was born in Florence, Italy and established a dressmaking salon at the turn of the twentieth century in Rome before moving her business to New York in 1919, specialized in dressmaker suits of fine tweeds and woolens. Renault often created clothing for New York society women as well as for some of the leading ladies of the Broadway stage. Marjorie's close friend Billie Burke may have introduced her to Renault, who created a number of tailored wool dresses for Marjorie to wear during her residency at Spaso House, the official residence of the American ambassador in Moscow. Marjorie ordered one striking, long-sleeve style in two colors. She had them custom-sized or tailored to fit her figure with her broad shoulders, small waist, and slim hips. These day dresses, costing approximately $225 each at that time, were the kind of heavy wool clothing she would need during her posting in Russia with her husband (see figs. 126, 127).

Joe was sworn in as Ambassador to the U.S.S.R. on November 22, 1936 in Washington, D.C. Part of FDR's instructions to him was to "befriend" the Russians, which meant lots of entertaining. As the diplomat's wife, much of this responsibility would naturally fall to Marjorie. "Mother loved to entertain," said Dina years later, "and here this was part of her job. She thought she'd died and gone to heaven."[6]

126
Day dress
Grey wool, dark grey braided
cotton cord
Rosie Renault, New York City, 1937
48.89

Day dress
Tan wool, dark brown braided
cotton cord
Rosie Renault, New York City, 1937
48.90

Marjorie ordered these tailored,
long-sleeved, wool dresses when
her husband was appointed the
United States ambassador to Soviet
Russia. As a representative of the
United States, Marjorie was very
conscious of her wardrobe in her new
diplomatic capacity. The simple lines
and adornments of decorative togs
on these dresses are a reflection of
Marjorie's desire to create a discreet
and sophisticated style as the wife of
an ambassador.

127
Detail of fig. 126

128
*Ambassador and Mrs.
Joseph E. Davies in
Moscow, 1937*

The Davies arrived in Moscow on January 19, 1937, after a transatlantic crossing on the *Europa* and a train ride to Moscow, with fifty pieces of hand luggage and thirty trunks. They, like other diplomats, were expected to use their personal household possessions for entertaining abroad, including fine china, crystal, and linens. Knowing that the Soviet Union had experienced severe food scarcities in 1933–34, and having been warned against eating dairy products, raw vegetables, rare meat, or products canned in Russia,[7] Marjorie arranged to have twelve food lockers of Birds Eye frozen foods plus two thousand pints of frozen cream shipped to Moscow on the *Sea Cloud* in advance of her arrival.[8]

Mindful of the fact that the Russians did not display their wealth after the fall of the tsar, Marjorie locked most of her jewelry in a safe and only took select diamond, sapphire, and pearl jewels with her to the Soviet Union. Yet she still dazzled the diplomatic corps with her ball gowns and dresses that were "more appropriate to the court of Versailles in 1750 than the Moscow embassy in 1937," said Emlen Knight Davies, Joe's youngest daughter from his former marriage, who had accompanied the couple to Russia. The wife of an embassy aide who met Marjorie in Moscow in 1937 described her as "the most stunning woman outside of *Harper's Bazaar.*"[9] Marjorie enchanted the Russians as well. "They were absolutely goggle-eyed," said Dina years later. "They'd never seen anything like that before. They looked at Mother with her clothes and jewels and [wondered] if the tsars had come back."[10]

Marjorie made the best of a challengingly cold climate, bundling up in heavy furs, high-top fur boots, fur hats, and fur muffs. She even wore fur coats inside Spaso House,

129
Evening dress
Black silk velvet backed with cotton
taffeta, faux pearls, rhinestones, silver
thread
Orry-Kelly, American, 1943
48.95
Designed by Hollywood costume
designer Orry-Kelly, this gown
was made for Marjorie's planned
on-screen appearance in the Warner
Bros. 1943 film *Mission to Moscow*.
The gown includes a finely detailed
bodice adorned with rhinestones
and silver metallic embroidery sewn
at the cap of the sleeves. The hem
is unfinished, a trick commonly used
to save time and money by movie
costume designers.

130
Detail of fig. 129

except in her bedroom, because temperatures in the large rooms of the ambassador's residence did not reach above fifty-five degrees.[11]

Despite the frigid cold conditions, being assigned to Russia proved to be a transformative opportunity. During their eighteen-month posting, in addition to carrying out their diplomatic duties, and establishing and expanding friendships in international circles, Marjorie and Joe ignited their passion for collecting Russian Imperial icons, liturgical vestments, and Fabergé. By the time of her death, Marjorie had assembled, with the help of a personal curator, one of the largest and most comprehensive collections of rare Russian Imperial *objets d'art* outside Russia. As Marjorie summarized in a long letter she wrote to First Lady Eleanor Roosevelt on March 17, 1938:

> Goodness, I am sorry to have gone on in book-fashion but I am so tremendously interested in what is going on around us here. It has, of course, been the greatest and most fascinating experience I have ever gone through in my life and I am always grateful for having the privilege of this opportunity.[12]

131
Marjorie Merriweather Post Davies
Oil on canvas 1946
Frank O. Salisbury (1874–1962)
England
51.43
Marjorie strikes an elegant pose wearing her sapphire and diamond necklace and earrings with a beautiful clip on the sweetheart neckline of her black velvet gown. A handsome sapphire ring accents her right hand.

After serving as Ambassador to the Soviet Union, Joe was appointed Ambassador to Belgium. The Davies arrived in Brussels in July of 1938. With war seeming imminent, however, Marjorie took Nedenia, who had joined them in Brussels, back to the States in October to attend school, and then rejoined Joe. But conditions worsened throughout the year. In August of 1939, while the Davies were vacationing at Topridge, Marjorie received orders not to return with her husband to Belgium, due to the dangerous conditions. By late 1939, Joe had resigned his ambassadorship and accepted a position in Washington, D.C. as special assistant to the Secretary of State.

The Hollywood glamour of the 1930s gave way to a new austerity with the outbreak of World War II. As women began taking on more responsibility during the war, the shoulders on their clothes got broader and more squared in the 1940s than in the 1930s, perhaps reflecting the extra burden women had to bear while the men in their families went to war. Due to wartime fabric shortages, hemlines were shortened, skirts narrowed, and sleeves tightened. In the summer of 1942, the United States War Production Board passed a mandatory regulation prohibiting pleats, ruffles, and patch pockets in an effort to conserve fabric.

When the Davies returned to the United States, they established their home in Washington, D.C., where Joe had lived for years and where Marjorie had spent her teen years while attending Mount Vernon Seminary. The couple rented a house on Foxhall Road

Opposite:

132

Marjorie Merriweather Post Davies at an evening event

Washington, D.C., ca. 1946

Marjorie is wearing the white beaded dress from Bergdorf Goodman in fig. 133.

This page:

133

Evening ensemble

White ground with blue floral pattern silk organza, white bugle beads

Bergdorf Goodman, New York City, 1946

48.154.1-3

This elegant evening gown features a matching short jacket.

134

Detail of fig. 133

135

Blue lapis purse

Maker Unknown, ca. 1935

2014.2.3

This velvet purse, with a clasp made of a carved lapis in the shape of a turtle dove and flower, is an elegant accessory of the mid-1930s. The inside of the purse is engraved Mrs. Marjorie Davies.

and entertained in grand style, hosting foreign diplomats, Supreme Court justices, senators, and high society. In 1941, Associated Press reporter Sigrid Arne wrote that Marjorie was the "most revered hostess in Washington."[13] That same year, the couple purchased Tregaron, a mansion on twenty acres in northwest Washington that they renovated before moving in during the spring of 1942. Mysteriously and unbeknownst to Marjorie, Joe had the title for Tregaron put in his name only.

After returning stateside, Joe wrote *Mission to Moscow*, a best-seller detailing his career as the former ambassador to the Soviet Union, which was published in December 1941. Warner Bros. adapted the book into a film and released it in 1943. While Hollywood actors Walter Huston and Ann Harding played Ambassador Davies and Marjorie in the movie, Joe personally appeared for an introduction to the film. Australian designer Orry-Kelly, chief costume designer at Warner Bros. between 1932 and 1944, had dressed actors including Ingrid Bergman, Bette Davis, and Katharine Hepburn, and later won three Oscars for Best Costume Design for *An American in Paris*, *Les Girls*, and *Some Like It Hot*. Orry-Kelly created all of the costumes for *Mission to Moscow*, including a wool suit for Joe to wear in his cameo and a black velvet gown for Marjorie to wear in a portrait to promote *Mission to Moscow* (see figs. 129, 130).

Orry-Kelly embellished the long-sleeve gown with rhinestones on the shoulders, pearl roping, and leaves embroidered with silver metal thread. Interestingly, this gown was never hemmed, and while many costumes created for Hollywood films were typically worn and then returned to wardrobe storage to be used in other films, this one found its way into Marjorie's closet. In fact, she liked it so much, Marjorie wore it for several portrait sittings, including one with Frank O. Salisbury in 1946. In that case, she accented the classic gown with a sapphire and diamond clip, placed strategically in the sweetheart neckline, and her stunning Cartier sapphire, diamond, and platinum necklace, with a fur draped over her shoulders (see fig. 131).

In the 1930s and 1940s, Marjorie often shopped along Fifth Avenue in New York City. Her favorite luxury department store was Bergdorf Goodman, where she had been a patron for more than forty years and where she had formed a friendship with the owner, Edwin Goodman. Bergdorf's had in-house designers working in a couture salon who created made-to-order clothing for their elite society clients. When Marjorie had fittings, her personal secretary, Margaret Voight, would phone in advance to arrange for her arrival at the 58th Street carriage entrance and once there, Marjorie would take the private elevator to the fourth floor, which was reserved for couture customers. Bergdorf Goodman had been the first American store to introduce ready-to-wear clothing in 1914, because Edwin Goodman was a visionary, yet it maintained a strong couture business as well. Marjorie would walk down a corridor lined with fresh flowers where she would be greeted by a receptionist at the end of the hall, who would use a small intercom system to alert Miss Gertrude, Marjorie's personal ladies wear clerk, of her arrival.[14]

136
Marjorie and Nedenia on Nedenia's wedding day
New York City, 1946

137
Evening dress
Peach with rose bouquet pattern brocade taffeta
Saks Fifth Avenue, New York City, 1946
48.94
Ordered along with her daughter Nedenia's wedding dress, Marjorie's mother-of-the-bride dress features a bustle-inspired ruffle at the back of the gown, a popular fashion trend in the 1940s.

138
Mother of the Bride hat
Saks Fifth Avenue, New York City, 1946
2012.9.21
Marjorie wore this ruffled pink hat to Nedenia's wedding in 1946.

Miss Gertrude would have requested additional staff for the fitting and reserved the largest fitting room, appointed with draperies and sheers on the big windows that overlooked Fifth Avenue, for Marjorie. Furnishings in the spacious fitting room included a small sofa with pillows, an upholstered chair, a tri-fold mirror, a coffee table, and plush rug. Sometimes ready-to-wear, or off-the-peg styles, would be presented to Marjorie to consider, other times she would request a custom design. On the occasions when fittings were long, a complimentary lunch of a half-sandwich and petite salad, or a croissant with fresh fruit, was served on white china. As Marjorie's schedule was very full, she reached a point where she did not have time to go to multiple fittings. She was such an important client that Bergdorf's had a dress form built to her exact measurements so fittings could be done in her absence.

During World War II, Marjorie worked with the American Red Cross, as she had during the Great War, and spoke out about the war, once to an audience of two thousand at a meeting of the Council of Soviet Relations.[15] Marjorie also leased *Sea Cloud* to the U.S. Navy for $1 per year from 1942 to 1945, since, as she said, she did not have a "son to give to the war."[16]

While she didn't have a son to send to war, Marjorie's daughter Dina volunteered to serve as an actress with the United Service Organizations. In 1945, Dina participated in a production of *The Man Who Came to Dinner* in the South Pacific. Marjorie was so worried about her daughter's safety that she went to extraordinary lengths to have letters and packages delivered to where she was stationed. At one point, one package was sent to Dina in Saipan. After the young actress opened it, she howled with laughter. "Dear Mom had sent me two rolls of toilet paper, which she was sure I didn't have out there, a box of Kleenex, and a girdle. With the girdle came a note: 'Do tell those fool jeep drivers not to drive too

141
Marjorie with husband, Joseph E. Davies, and stepdaughter, Eleanor (Emlen) Knight Davies
1947
Marjorie, in an evening gown from Bonwit Teller (fig. 142) shares a laugh with her husband and stepdaughter.

142
Evening dress
Satin, taffeta faille
Bonwit Teller, New York City, 1947
48.101.1-2
After World War II, evening dresses moved away from the form fitting and columnar silhouette to fuller, more sweeping skirts and fitted bodices. This look emphasized the figure of the mature woman by highlighting the bust, waist, and hips.

fast, and wear this because it will bounce your insides out if you don't.'"[17] Thankfully, World War II ended in 1945, and life regained some normalcy.

On March 26, 1946, Dina wore a classically elegant wedding gown from Saks Fifth Avenue when she married Stanley Rumbough Jr. "Miss Hutton made an exquisite picture as a bride … her blonde loveliness was set off by her white satin gown … with off-the-shoulder neckline and white satin flowers embroidered with pearls," noted *The New York Times* on its society pages. Marjorie's salmon brocade taffeta dress, also from Saks, featured leg-of-mutton sleeves (see figs. 136–138). Now a world-class hostess, Marjorie had outdone herself with the wedding arrangements. Years later, Dina said of her mother, "She created the whole thing! She was amazing. She organized the entire wedding. She was like a stage manager in a theater."[18]

In 1947, Christian Dior launched his first collection with the "New Look," which marked a radical departure from the more masculine, understated fashions prevalent at the end of the war. Dior proposed longer skirts, beautifully finished on the inside with seams reinforced by tapes to make them stand away from the body and hemlines as low as twelve inches from the ground with tiny corseted waists, snug bodices, and rounded, sloping shoulders. His ultra-feminine designs usually mixed natural and synthetic fibers, which had been perfected during the war.[19] The style that Dior created brought femininity back to fashion. Marjorie embraced the elegant lines of the "New Look." The style was well suited to her corseted figure, narrow waist, and slim hips.

The following year on March 19, Marjorie was chairman of the "New Look Ball" for the Everglades Club and helped raise $176,000 on behalf of the Good Samaritan Hospital. Wallis Simpson headed one of the fundraiser's subcommittees. A few days later, she and her husband, the Duke of Windsor, boarded the *Sea Cloud* to cruise with Marjorie and Joe. The Duke of Windsor later sent a note to Joe that said:

143
Dinner dress
Grey silk taffeta, cut steel, glass
beads
Bonwit Teller, New York City, ca. 1948
48.100
Marjorie embraced Christian Dior's
"New Look" when she selected this
dinner dress with a cinched waist, full
skirt, and broad, padded shoulders.

144
Detail of fig. 143

145
Evening dress
Black silk taffeta, black tulle, black silk taffeta/acetate, net, horsehair
Maker Unknown, American, ca. 1948
48.105.1-3
This dress with rounded shoulders and a V-neckline illustrates the change to a fuller silhouette taking place at the end of the 1940s.

146
Detail of fig. 145

147
Black purse and coin purse
Coin Purse: Cartier, Paris, France
49.7
Black Purse: Unknown maker
2014.6.9
Marjorie ordered the black purse adorned with a metal "MDP" monogram when she married Joseph E. Davies in 1935. She bought the coin purse, which is decorated in an art deco geometric pattern, in 1925.

148
Evening dress
Silk brocade with bands of grey, green, tan, and copper with black paisley pattern
Eleanora Garnett, Italy, ca. 1950
48.103
This full length evening dress is made in a silk brocade fabric with wide color bands of grey-green, tan, and copper with an overall matte black paisley pattern.

149
Evening dress
Silk satin brocade with floral pattern
Bonwit Teller, New York City, ca. 1950
48.104
As the 1940s came to a close and a new decade emerged, rich, vivid colors made an appearance in garments both for day and evening wear. This gown of bright blue and pink brocade illustrates this shift in the color palette of Marjorie's wardrobe.

Opposite:
150
Marjorie at Mar-a-Lago
ca. 1950

151
Ball gown
Cream silk taffeta, green tulle, cotton canvas
Hattie Carnegie, Inc., New York City, ca. 1950
48.87
This ball gown was purchased only a few years before Hattie Carnegie's death. By this time, the Carnegie name had become legendary in American fashion. Marjorie's support of American designers continued to gain momentum through the decade.

Opposite:
152
Marjorie stepping out of a car
Europe, ca. 1950
Marjorie wearing a floral day dress with hydrangea patterns complemented with hat, gloves and a wrap as she stepped out of a car in Europe.

153
Dinner dress
Black woven net, dark blue velvet, black taffeta
Oldric Royce, Inc., New York City, ca. 1950
48.116.1-2
Oldric Royce was Marjorie's favorite designer from the late 1940s through the 1960s.

Words are quite inadequate in trying to thank you and Mrs. Davies for the wonderful time you gave us … the Duchess and I could not have enjoyed the cruise more, whether at sea especially under sail or ashore in Nassau and Havana. It was an ideal combination of rest and quiet and then the interest and excitement of visiting the historic and picturesque capital of Cuba for the first time. You are both perfect hosts and I derived great stimulation from our talks … Your charming hospitality will always be a high spot in my memories.[20]

Back in Washington, D.C., Ruth Buchanan and her husband Wiley Buchanan Jr., who became the American ambassador to Luxembourg and later to Austria, admired the couple's gracious entertaining as well. "They loved to dance and along the way, I made their

acquaintance," said Ruth, who, with Wiley, invited the Davies to their home, Underoak, a lovely English Tudor estate in northwest Washington. "It was our ninth anniversary in 1949 and we had a party on a beautiful day in April. I felt so proud to have Marjorie and Joe in my home and they were excited about the gardens." At that time, Marjorie was forming a dance group and the Buchanans volunteered to host an evening in their home. "We fed them dinner in our dining room and then we went to the ballroom and we had an orchestra, and we just danced. We had about 30 guests … I remember watching her dance on the new floor and she looked so magnificent," Ruth remembered. "Marjorie was perfection to me and my husband," Ruth said. "Wiley would say, 'I'm going to make you the next Marjorie.' She was just like a model, she was a beautiful hostess, and she dressed immaculately. My husband was directing that I should be just like that."[21] In fact, Marjorie mentored Ruth the same way Eva Stotesbury had mentored her years earlier in Palm Beach.

When the Buchanans were posted to Luxembourg, Marjorie visited and stayed with the family. Dede Wilsey, the Buchanans' daughter, remembers one visit when Marjorie let her try on her Cartier emerald necklace:

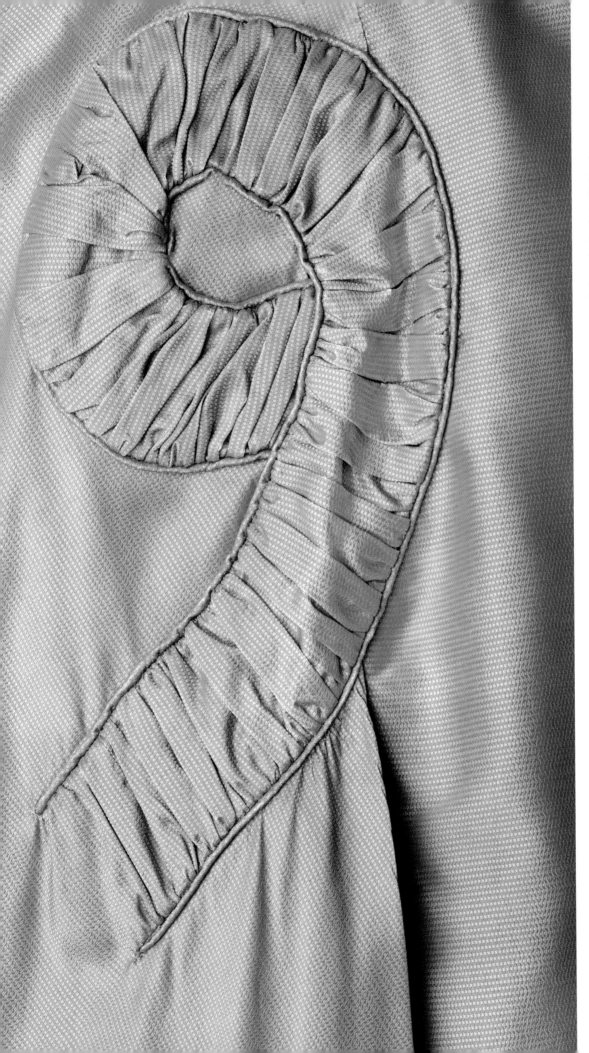

154
Evening gown
Silver waffle weave silk faille
Ann Lowe, New York City, 1952
48.106
Marjorie wore this gown by African
American designer Ann Lowe for her
portrait by artist Douglas Chandor.
A year after Marjorie purchased
this dress, Jacqueline Bouvier gave
a boost of recognition to Lowe
when the designer custom made
the wedding gown for her marriage
to John Fitzgerald Kennedy. The
swirl-like motifs on this dress are
characteristic of Lowe's work.

155
Detail of fig. 154

One thing about Marjorie is she'd let you try her jewelry on. She knew I loved jewelry and she knew I loved clothes. That was so much fun for a little girl. She was very thoughtful that way. Of course, she had fabulous posture, absolutely ramrod straight, no matter what. When she was staying in Luxembourg with us, Mother and Daddy were having a dance in her honor and she had her big emeralds on. I was in her bedroom and she said, "Do you want to see my dress twirl?" And I said, "Oh yes, I'd love that," I was about 10 … I can see it today … There were yards and yards of printed chiffon with a white and green print with big emeralds … She always had the jewelry match the gown exactly.

At home in Washington, the Davies ran a formal household, even when it was just the two of them. Gustav Modig, known as "Mr. Gus," who began working for Marjorie in 1948 as a footman at Mar-a-Lago and rose to become majordomo at Hillwood in Washington, recalled years later that Joe dressed for dinner in a tuxedo each night and Marjorie wore a tea gown with a train. "That was—a train from here to there in the tea gown. I mean, that was also something I had never seen in other houses," Gus said.

On the home front, Joe's influence in the political world had begun to wane during the war and in the interim he had become extremely possessive of Marjorie, and at times overbearing. With his failing career and his failing health, tensions mounted, nerves were frayed, and the Davies' marriage began to unravel. By this stage in her life, Marjorie was self-assured enough to know she did not want to continue in her present situation. She moved out of Tregaron to a hotel and began to look for a house to buy to make her own home.

During the Davies' separation, Eleanor Close Barzin, Marjorie's second daughter, asked her mother to consider having her portrait painted by the renowned English portraitist Douglas Chandor, who had also been commissioned by Queen Elizabeth II, President Franklin D. Roosevelt, First Lady Eleanor Roosevelt, and Sir Winston Churchill. Eleanor said, "I wanted Mummy to have her portrait painted by Chandor because of his reputation and she wasn't interested and said 'no.' So I bargained with her and asked if she would have it done for me as two birthday gifts and two Christmas gifts and she agreed."[22]

In 1952, Marjorie purchased a beautiful silvery/grey silk faille evening gown with a sweetheart neckline and intricate trapunto detailing created by Ann Lowe, an African American designer from Alabama who had worked for various fashion houses before establishing her own dress salon in Manhattan in 1950. Lowe was the same designer who created many dresses for the Auchincloss family, including the wedding gown that Jacqueline Bouvier wore when she married John F. Kennedy the following year.[23] Marjorie's Ann Lowe gown was immortalized when she wore it to sit for Chandor (see figs. 154–156).

The Chandor portrait reflects Marjorie's quintessential style. At sixty-five, she looks regal in her elegant gown and exquisite jewels with lace draped over one arm, fur under the other, and an orchid, her favorite flower, in her right hand. Chandor captured the exact shade of blue of her eyes, and this portrait became one of Marjorie's favorites.

156
Marjorie Merriweather Post
Oil on canvas, 1952
Douglas Chandor (1897–1953)
51.156
This portrait is unfinished because painter Douglas Chandor died before he could complete it. Marjorie's daughter Eleanor, who commissioned the painting, accepted the portrait unfinished and later donated it to Hillwood, stating that it was an excellent likeness of her mother.

Endnotes

1 Marjoe Cruise 1935–36, *Sea Cloud* vol. 2, Hillwood Collection.

2 Ibid.

3 Nancy Rubin, *American Empress: The Life and Times of Marjorie Merriweather Post* (New York: Villard Books, 1995), 216.

4 Ibid., 219.

5 Dina Merrill, interview, June 6, 2006, Oral history, Hillwood Collection.

6 Rubin, *American Empress*, 220.

7 William Wright, *Heiress: The Rich Life of Marjorie Merriweather Post* (Washington, D.C.: New Republic Books, 1978), 133.

8 Rubin, *American Empress*, 223.

9 Ibid., 222.

10 Ibid., 222–23.

11 Wright, *Heiress*, 134.

12 Eleanor Roosevelt Personal Papers, 100. Personal Correspondence at the Franklin Delano Roosevelt Library at Hyde Park.

13 Rubin, *American Empress*, 266.

14 Betty Halbreich (Bergdorf Goodman Personal Shopper), interview by Howard Kurtz, June 16, 2014, Oral history, Hillwood Collection; and Marjorie Post's telephone book, ca. 1960.

15 Wright, *Heiress*, 170.

16 Rubin, *American Empress* 276.

17 Ibid., 277.

18 Interview, *Wedding Belles* (Fall 2010), Hillwood Collection.

19 J. Anderson Black and Madge Garland, *A History of Fashion*, updated and revised by Frances Kennett (New York: William Morrow and Company, 1980), 248.

20 Rubin, *American Empress*, 300–301.

21 Ruth Buchanan, interview by Patricia Donnally, May 18, 2014.

22 "The Chandor Portrait of Mrs. Post," conversation with Carol Warner, January 1992, Hillwood Collection.

23 Margaret Powell, 'The Remarkable Story of Ann Lowe: From Alabama to Madison Avenue', http://blogs.archives.gov/prologue/?p=11922 (accessed August 6, 2014).

A GRANDE DAME OF SOCIETY AND THE END OF AN ERA

1955–1973

Feeling strong, confident, and independent, Marjorie purchased a glorious twenty five-acre estate with a thirty five-room Georgian mansion overlooking Rock Creek Park in Washington, D.C. With her inimitable style, excellent organizational skills, and exceptional vision, she set out to make it a place to call home. She resumed using her maiden name, Marjorie Merriweather Post, after divorcing Joe in 1955, and spent two years having her new residence, which she named Hillwood, renovated to her exacting standards.

Marjorie gave a glimpse into her exquisite new world when she posed for *Vogue* in her elegant white and gold French drawing room at Hillwood. She wore a sculptural custom gown with a silver silk satin bodice and attached dark grey silk faille skirt known as "The Clover," designed by the innovative Anglo-American couturier Charles James. Despite protests from James, Marjorie embellished her gown with her Cartier brooch, a waterfall of emeralds cascading from the bodice, and her Indian-style emerald necklace. The famous German fashion photographer Horst P. Horst exquisitely captured Marjorie in her new milieu. The image ran in the November issue of *Vogue* in 1957 (see p. 130).

That same autumn, Marjorie was awarded the cross of a Chevalier of the Legion of Honor. French ambassador Hervé Alphand presented her with the award at the French Embassy in Washington, D.C., praising Marjorie for her "long demonstrated friendship towards France." Not only had Marjorie established the 3,000-bed Number 8 Base Hospital at Savenay during World War I, she had also raised funds for the Versailles Exposition on the bicentennial anniversary of Marie Antoinette's birthday in 1955.[1] Marjorie wore a gown with a dark plum silk velvet bodice and a pink taffeta faille skirt to the celebratory dinner (fig. 159). Scooped necklines and various embellishments made pinning the medal on the left side of her formal wear a bit challenging, especially since the medal would swing when she leaned forward. As she told Jenny Mattson, her cook and pastry chef, after one dinner where she wore the medal, "It damn near fell in the soup." She

157
Marjorie Merriweather Post receiving the French Legion of Honor
Washington, D.C., 1957
French ambassador Hervé Alphand presented Marjorie with the cross of Chevalier of the Legion of Honor on October 31, 1957.

158
Chevalier of the Legion of Honor Medal
18.78.1
Marjorie received France's highest award, given in appreciation of her "long-demonstrated friendship towards France."

Previous page:
Marjorie at Hillwood
Photograph: Horst ©Vogue
1957
Photographed for the 1957 issue of *Vogue* magazine, Marjorie appeared confident and relaxed in the French drawing room of her new Washington, D.C. home, Hillwood. She wore "The Clover," a custom-designed gown by Anglo-American couturier Charles James.

159
Evening dress
Purple silk velvet, pink taffeta, purple acetate, pink nylon net
Eleanora Garnett, Italy, 1957
48.107
Marjorie received many honors and accolades throughout her life for her charitable work. This is the gown she wore when she received the French Legion of Honor (fig. 157).

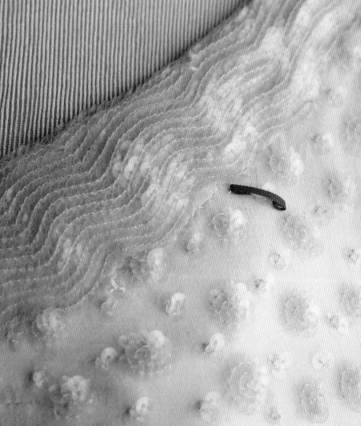

160
Evening dress
Cream silk crêpe, cream
nylon organza, cream chiffon,
iridescent sequins
Oldric Royce, Inc., New York City,
1962
48.115.1-2
Marjorie wore this "mermaid"
dress to the opening of the New
York Philharmonic at Lincoln
Center for the Performing Arts
in September 1962.

161
Detail of fig. 160
The official red ribbon sewn onto
Marjorie's gown denoting her French
Legion of Honor award.

162

Dinner dress
Red silk taffeta, machine-made lace
printed with yellow and black design
Bonwit Teller, New York City,
ca. 1955
48.108.1-2
By the 1950s the growth of off-the-
rack fashions grew exponentially.
Nevertheless, Marjorie continued to
have much of her wardrobe custom
made. This dress was a special design
from the high-end department store
Bonwit Teller, known at the time for
its promotion of French designers.

163

Marjorie in dinner dress
Palm Beach, Florida, ca. 1955
For an evening out, Marjorie wore a
ballerina-length dinner dress popular
in the mid-1950s (fig. 164). The
dress is accompanied by a short fur
jacket and her Cartier sapphire and
diamond necklace.

164

Dinner dress
White net, lavender tulle, lavender
taffeta faille, white corded lace,
iridescent white sequins
Town-Travel Wear Ltd., Waldorf
Astoria, New York City, ca. 1955
48.110
Marjorie purchased this dinner dress
from Town-Travel Wear Ltd., a design
salon that was then in the Waldorf
Astoria Hotel.

discovered that the custom of wearing a delicate red ribbon sewn onto her evening wear to symbolize the medal was easier than wearing the actual medal (see fig. 161).

Marjorie considered dancing a form of exercise and she danced her whole life. By the 1950s, square dancing had become so popular that she integrated it into her entertaining in all of her homes. Marjorie became famous for her "round and square dances," which alternated classic ballroom dancing with square dancing. No one wanted to miss her square dances, including Rose Kennedy, who after attending one at Mar-a-Lago, sent a thank you note expressing, "I have not had so many attractive dancing partners since I was a debutante."[2] Marjorie would even bring in Arthur Murray's school of professional dancers to help guide any guests who might not know the steps. Naturally, she had dozens of square

165
Square dance blouse
White cotton
ca. 1950
2013.5.6
For her hallmark square dances,
Marjorie often wore a neutral colored
cotton blouse with, a brightly colored
skirt, and multi-layered petticoats.
Colored Mexican Square Dance Skirt
Beige linen with painted motif in
primary colors, black cotton, silver
metal sequins
Tipicano Mexicanos, Mexico, ca. 1950
2013.5.10
Marjorie often wore skirts with
Mexican designs during square
dancing events. This painted skirt
may have been purchased on a trip
to Mexico.

166
*Marjorie dancing the tango with
partner*
1962
Marjorie, who dominated both
ballroom and square dancing,
demonstrated the tango at a charity
fundraiser in 1962.

dancing costumes consisting of a simple short-sleeve white blouse and a stiff cotton skirt
with layers of colorful petticoats beneath, completed by her stylish dancing shoes (fig. 165).

Marjorie could tango as well. "I remember my grandmother being so great at the tango
and always holding the floor when the musicians would take a break from playing. The
record player would come on and she always used to demonstrate the tango for everyone,"
said Nina Rumbough, Dina's daughter.[3] Marjorie once held a room spellbound when she
tangoed with John D. Rockefeller while vacationing at the Homestead in Virginia.[4]

During the late 1950s, Herbert May, an executive vice president of Westinghouse Air
Brake International who lived in Pittsburgh Pennsylvania, and traveled to Washington
frequently for business, had become one of Marjorie's steady escorts. The handsome, silver-

167
Marjorie in a grey dress by Martha,
Inc. with Alexander Matsas, Greek
Ambassador to the United States
Palm Beach, Florida, ca. 1955
Photograph: Bert Morgan Studios

168
Evening dress
Cream taffeta, green silk organza,
clear rhinestones
Copied by Oldric Royce, Inc., New
York City, ca. 1955
48.113
Marjorie ordered this off-the-
shoulder evening dress in both
grey and green. The design
complemented her classic, mature
sense of style.

haired widower shared much in common with Marjorie, including mutual friends and a love of dancing and entertaining.

On one occasion, Herbert told friends he had fallen in love with Marjorie and mentioned how beautiful she had looked in a dress that perfectly matched the color of her eyes. Dina recalled later that when her mother told her this story, Marjorie pointed out that the color of the dress she had worn that evening was dark purple. Several months later, when Marjorie was preparing to marry Herb, she asked Oldric Royce to create a ballerina length, blue lace dress the exact blue of her eyes to wear for her wedding (see fig. 169). "I wanted to make an honest man out of him," she told Dina.[7]

Marjorie married Herb on June 23, 1958 at Adelaide's country home in Maryland. The following day, her granddaughter Ellen, stationed in a Texas army camp with her new husband, George Iverson, cabled her best wishes to her seventy one-year-old grandmother. Marjorie wired back, "Walking on fluffy pink clouds."[8]

The Mays took eighty pieces of luggage on the Swedish cruise ship *Gripsholm* for their honeymoon, which lasted a couple of months. They traveled to Iceland, Norway, Finland, Austria, Switzerland, France, and England. Mr. Gus, Marjorie's butler, and two young

Opposite:

169

Wedding dress

Pale blue silk acetate, pale blue
corded lace, pale blue net

Oldric Royce, Inc., New York City,
1958

48.111

Marjorie had her wedding dress
custom made to match the blue
color of her eyes, which her groom,
Herbert May, greatly admired.

170

*Marjorie and Herbert May at their
wedding reception*

Pittsburgh, Pennsylvania, June 23,
1958

171

Dinner dress

Yellow silk acetate, nude silk organza,
green net

Oldric Royce, Inc., New York City,
ca. 1960

48.151

This short dress of bright yellow and
green is a variation of her blue 1958
wedding dress.

Marjorie purchased multiple copies
of her favorite dresses throughout
throughout her life.

172

Detail of fig. 171

This page:

173

Evening dress

Pink silk satin with purple and silver
metallic thread brocade

Oldric Royce, Inc., New York City,
ca. 1960

48.117.1-2

This draped dress is reminiscent of
the gown Marjorie wore to receive
the French Legion of Honor award
(see fig. 159).

personal maids went along to help and had a cabin on the boat for the many trunks and
pieces of luggage, as well as Marjorie's ironing board.[9]

Her philanthropic activities kept Marjorie very busy during the late 1950s. She
established the "Music for Young America" program, an annual series of thirty concerts
for children, for the National Symphony Orchestra, which she single-handedly financed.
She donated a new Georgian Colonial red brick building to her alma mater, the Mount
Vernon Seminary and Junior College.[10] Marjorie also became very involved in establishing
the Washington Ballet Guild, hosting teas and receptions at Hillwood. She donated nine
of her own gowns as costumes for a 1958 Christmas performance of *The Nutcracker* at
Constitution Hall.[11] "She was on a lot of boards," said Ellen, her granddaughter. "She
was very involved with the cultural life in this city."[12] In 1958, Marjorie became director
emeritus of the General Foods Corporation. She was the first woman to be decorated by

the Boy Scouts of America and was largely responsible for the establishment of its Service Center in Washington (fig. 174).[13]

As the active septuagenarian's numerous social commitments called for many beautiful clothes, Marjorie began to engage Oldric Royce more frequently. In fact, the New York-based designer became her favorite. Around 1949, Marjorie began to commission Oldric Royce to make dresses for her. Born Oldrich Rosenbaum in 1896 in Prague, he immigrated to the United States in 1939 in the wake of the Nazi annexation of Czechoslovakia, leaving behind a successful dressmaking business in Prague. He changed his name when he reached America and set up shop at 16 East 52nd Street in New York City, where he designed made-to-order styles for private clients, including Marlene Dietrich, Ginger Rogers, Ethel Merman, and Happy Rockefeller. Royce grew to become one of Marjorie's favorite designers. His feminine fashions with cinched waists and elegant lines were the kinds of styles that appealed to her. His exquisite creations were as meticulously finished on the inside as on the outside. Royce became an American citizen in 1944. He received a patent for a shoulder pad invention he called the "Shoulder Perfectioner" in 1946. In the early 1950s, Royce won the Grand Prize in the American Fashion Competitions, sponsored by *The Chicago Tribune*. His reputation grew and soon he was designing fashions for First Ladies Bess Truman and Mamie Eisenhower, as well as the movie stars he counted as clients. Marjorie felt that Royce effortlessly translated her mature elegant style into dresses and gowns that suited her to perfection. Sometimes, if Marjorie especially liked a certain style, she would order the same design in different colors. And she didn't have to go to Royce for fittings; he would travel to her wherever she was. By the time she died, Marjorie owned

179
Marjorie in a yellow and cream day dress and jacket
Location Unknown, ca. 1960
Photograph: Bert Morgan Studio
Marjorie also purchased the same ensemble in bright green and cream from Oldric Royce (fig. 180).

180
Day dress with jacket
Raw silk, green wool crêpe, cream silk, cream acetate
Oldric Royce, Inc., New York City, ca. 1960
48.127.1-4
Marjorie primarily wore day dresses with matching short jackets when conducting business affairs. As with formal dresses, she purchased the same outfit in multiples, as is the case of this ensemble ordered in both green and yellow.

181
Photo without jacket of fig. 180

182
Detail of white or alternate green buttons of fig. 180

183
Evening dress
Pink organza, black lace, pink taffeta,
black velvet, pink net
Oldric Royce, Inc., New York City,
ca. 1960
48.118
This striking evening gown has much
in common with the dinner dress in
fig. 184. The dress has a distinctive
bold diamond pattern and a minutely
pleated skirt.

184
Dinner dress
White organza, grey and pink lace,
pink taffeta, pink net
Oldric Royce, Inc., New York City,
ca. 1960
48.119.1-4
Similar to the evening dress in fig.
183, this diamond patterned dress
of white organza with grey and
pink lace has a beautiful accordion
pleated skirt.

185
Lady Bird Johnson and Marjorie Merriweather Post
Mar-A-Lago, Florida, 1968

186
Day suit
Grey and white silk faille on yellow
ground
Béla Ross at Oldric Royce, Inc., New
York City, tailored by Tony Abate,
ca. 1960
48.128
Mature and sophisticated women
often wore fitted suits while going
about their daytime business. The
bright colors and bold geometric
patterns are notable stylistic
elements of the early 1960s.

187
Detail of fig. 186

Opposite:

188
Evening dress and evening jacket ensemble
Bright blue silk, clear rhinestones, silver sequins, clear glass beads, faux pearls, silver nylon lace
Rizik Bros. Inc., Washington, D.C., ca. 1960
2012.1.5
Marjorie especially enjoyed wearing princess style, A-line gowns. These three custom-made gowns with different embellishments and design details that distinguish them. This striking turquoise evening dress has a matching floor-length coat trimmed with silver lace.

189
Evening gown
Yellow silk bengaline, silk organza, silk soutache
Oldric Royce, Inc.,
New York City, ca. 1960
2012.1.4
This yellow sleeveless gown features Chinese knots on the bodice and around the skirt.

190
Evening gown
Green silk taffeta flocked with chenille
Béla Ross at Oldric Royce, Inc., New York City, tailored by Tony Abate, ca. 1960
2012.1.3
This green silk taffeta dress includes a capelet.

191
Blue shoes
Bob Shoes, Inc., New York City, 1950–1970
49.38.1-2, 49.44.1-2, 49.46.1-2
Marjorie liked to buy multiple copies of her accessories in different colors. For example, she ordered three "Alice" style shoes, named after Alice Roosevelt and known for their ankle straps with horizontal cut designs, in various shades of blue.

192
Pastel shoes
Bob Shoes, Inc., New York City, 1950–1970
49.66.1-2, 49.74.1-2, 49.63.1-2, & 49.67.1-2
Marjorie had her shoes custom made by Bob Shoes, Inc. "The Diamond" style features a T-strap and diamond cutouts on the vamp. She ordered them in an array of pastel shades.

This page:

193
Marjorie with four grandchildren
Palm Beach, Florida, ca. 1961
Marjorie is seen here wearing a bright green dress from Béla Ross at Oldric Royce, Inc., (fig. 190) with four of her grandchildren at Mar-a-Lago.

dozens of elegant dresses, gowns, and suits by Royce (see figs. 176, 177, 178, 180, 183, 184, 186, 189, 190, 193).

Royce would accommodate Marjorie and send a swatch of the fabric he was using for a particular dress to Bob Shoes, Inc. to be sure her handmade shoes would match precisely. The shoes were created in one of two styles. They were either "The Alice," named after Alice Roosevelt, which included an ankle strap and openings on the vamp that first became popular between 1920 and 1930, or they were "The Diamond," a T-strap style that featured diamond cutouts on the sides of the shoe near the ankle and on the vamp. Marjorie had shoes in almost every color, especially various shades of blue, including robin's egg, seafoam, turquoise, steel, and navy (figs. 191, 192). She even had custom-made hard-soled slippers with heels that featured the flags of *Sea Cloud* done in needlepoint.

Marjorie's accessories matched her clothes. "Marjorie Merriweather Post dropped in with a satchel full of jewels. She asked for dresses to match; green chiffon for the emeralds, pink for the rubies, and white for the diamonds," said Lynn Manulis, the daughter of Martha Philips, who owned the Martha salons in New York City and Palm Beach.[14]

Stylish hats were *de rigueur* for a proper lady during the early 1960s and Marjorie enjoyed wearing hats so much that she had the roof of her 1964 Cadillac series 75 limousine raised five inches over her passenger seat to accommodate her chapeaux.[15] Esther Kirwan Steck, a Washington, D.C. based milliner, made dozens of Marjorie's hats, as well as hats for the wives of many senators and congressmen (see fig. 194).[16]

Victoria G. Petrini, a dressmaker originally from Florence, Italy, who established dressmaking salons in Florence and Rome before moving to Washington in 1929, sewed and did alterations for Marjorie. She made her golf outfits and summer day dresses, among

194
Flower hat in plastic box
Kirwan Steck, ca. 1960
2012.9.43

other garments. Petrini counted First Lady Mamie Eisenhower, Pamela Harriman, and Dina Merrill among her clients as well.

Marjorie also had many beautiful handbags, some with her initials. She even carried an evening bag for dinners in her own home. While she never handled cash, she needed a handbag for personal essentials such as lipstick or a tissue.

Just as she had her dresses, shoes, and hats custom-tailored, Marjorie had a customized beauty ritual as well. When she was having Hillwood renovated, in addition to having her home designed to beautifully display her collections of Russian Imperial treasures and her French *objets d'art*, she had her bedroom suite designed to accommodate all of her grooming needs. Marjorie's dressing room, complete with a fireplace, featured her desk overlooking the French parterre. Her vanity included a built-in button she could press to signal her personal maid Eva Zackrisson as she was finishing her toilette. Marjorie had her bathroom decorated in pink, her favorite color. She even had a pink tub installed, reflecting the national craze for "First Lady Pink," which became popular after Mamie Eisenhower selected a pink inaugural gown.

One luxury, perfect for pampering, was the massage/hairdressing room with a massage table and oils that Marjorie had set up near her bedroom. Joe Hand, her masseur, would give Marjorie massages in this room, which featured scores of black-and-white, sepia tone, and color photos of family and friends, plus a shampoo sink in the corner. Hairdressing equipment was pulled out each Thursday. On this day, Steward Bankert, owner of The Kut 'N Kurl in Sykesville, Maryland, would close his shop and go to Hillwood from 8 a.m. until 4 p.m.[17]

Bankert used the health-conscious Harper Method, created by Martha Matilda Harper, a Christian Scientist, in the late nineteenth century. Harper's technique involved not only washing the hair, but also massaging the scalp, neck, and shoulders to stimulate blood flow and help hair grow.[18] It also involved using rainwater, so Marjorie had a reservoir built on Hillwood's roof to collect water, which would then flow into a filtration system and heating tank. The rainwater was piped to the hairdressing salon to be used on her long, thick hair. Marjorie's hair reached below her waist by the time she died. Bankert would perm Marjorie's hair about three times a year and the process would take all day. Once, Bankert suggested that Marjorie could simplify things by having her hair cut. Marjorie responded:

> No. I see all these women. They can't go out unless they have an appointment with the beauty shop that afternoon. I can go anytime I want and I don't have to worry. I just take my hair and twist it up and go. Otherwise, I'd have to be going, having it all teased and fluffed up and all—I don't have that much time.[19]

It's true, Marjorie was on the move; she and Herb would travel from Hillwood to Mar-a-Lago and Camp Topridge regularly. And no matter where she was, Marjorie entertained in elegant style. "Of course at dinner we were dressed with tuxedos, formal, even in the middle of the mountains," described guest Walter Beach, adding that footmen in [black] tie, jacket, and cummerbund served dinner.[20]

"You wanted to take your best of everything," said Betty Beale, society editor of

195
Evening suit
Pale blue raw silk satin, pink silk acetate, white glass beads, clear plastic beads, white fur, pink satin
Béla Ross at Oldric Royce, Inc., New York City, tailored by Tony Abate, ca. 1960
48.124.1-2

196
Detail of fig. 195

197
Evening dress with jacket
Pale blue silk satin with flocked dark blue velvet floral pattern, blue and white ostrich feathers
Béla Ross at Oldric Royce, Inc., New York City, tailored by Tony Abate, ca. 1960
48.123.1-2
Evoking the eclecticism of the late 1950s and early 1960s, this two-piece evening dress and jacket are both "flocked," a technique that creates a raised motif on fabric. The jacket sleeves are trimmed with blue and white ostrich feathers.

198
Detail of fig. 197

199
Fig. 197 without jacket

Washington's *Evening Star* and a syndicated columnist in ninety newspapers nationwide, referring to returning guests who knew the staff would unpack their clothes and put everything away for them. In fact, when visitors to one of Marjorie's homes prepared to leave, her valets would repack their bags with the clothes cleaned and pressed and tissue paper placed between garments to prevent wrinkles.[21]

If guests wanted to visit with Marjorie privately at Camp Topridge, they had to make an appointment. Beale remembered one meeting with Marjorie:

> Whatever the cause of my visit to her lodge, our talk turned to such feminine things as a one-piece, form-fitting garment to wear under strapless evening gowns. As Mrs. Post, even in her senior years, had almost the same measurements as I, including a twenty-six-inch waist, she suggested I try on the lace and elastic pink job she had made for her. So I put on the beautiful, sexy garment and also began trying on her fabulous jewels that she brought out for the fun of it. In no time I had wreathed my neck and wrists in diamonds and other precious stones and pinned to every inch of the front of the pink and lace job a fortune in jewels. To Marjorie's amusement I viewed myself in a full-length mirror with pleasure from every angle before returning the gems and the strapless unmentionable.[22]

In 1963, insurmountable difficulties arose between Marjorie and Herb. The following year, Marjorie divorced him and resumed using her maiden name. The mid-1960s brought many changes, especially in fashion. While other women were wearing miniskirts, donning trousers, and in some cases burning their bras, Marjorie stayed true to her classic style. She knew exactly who she was and what she did and did not like. As her granddaughter Ellen recalled with a laugh:

> She did not like it when the skirts got short and the stockings got white. I got called down for that. "Those skirts are too short, and the stockings are terrible, dear." You know, it was very in in the '60s. I mean Jackie Kennedy was wearing them, so we all wore short skirts and white stockings. Grandmother didn't approve of that at all.

Ladies were not permitted to wear trousers in Marjorie's homes either. "The only one really that wore slacks, or trousers was Ms. Deenie (Dina Merrill)," said Mr. Gus.[24] Once, Dina came home from Hollywood and brought six pairs of pantyhose with her in a box. She handed them to Marjorie and said, "Mother, these are going to change your life." Marjorie took the pantyhose out, stretched them over her hands, then folded them neatly, and placed them back in the box. She handed them back to Dina and said, "No dear, these are going to change *your* life." Marjorie wasn't looking for emancipation from her corset, she was looking for support. She was perfectly happy wearing stockings with garters, which had served her well for decades.

200
Marjorie at Hillwood
Washington, D.C., ca. 1960
Photograph: Arnold Newman
Always fond of drama and
theatricality, Marjorie posed at
Hillwood in a red velvet dress with
long, bat sleeves. Reigning as the
"Grand Dame" of the nation's capital,
Marjorie's clothes evoked a sense
of grandeur and authority in her
later years.

Opposite:
201
*Marjorie at a celebration in honor
of Queen Elizabeth II*
British ambassador's residence,
Washington, D.C., ca. 1960
Marjorie is talking to guests at an
outdoor celebration. She is wearing
a hat and holding a parasol.

202
Hats
Kirwan Steck, ca. 1960
2012.9.30, 2012.9.32
Hats were essential accessories for
all of Marjorie's afternoon outfits in
the 1950s and early 1960s.

203
Flower parasol
Maker Unknown, ca. 1960
2014.11.14
Made of modern synthetic materials,
this parasol is a prime example of
umbrellas and parasols of the 1950s
and 1960s with bright floral patterns
and thick plastic handles.

204
*Marjorie Merriweather Post on her
80th birthday*
Washington, D.C., 1967
At Marjorie's eightieth birthday
celebration at Constitution Hall
in Washington, D.C., the National
Symphony honored her for her
philanthropic support of the arts.

On March 15, 1967, to celebrate her eightieth birthday, Marjorie's son-in-law Leon Barzin flew in from Paris with wife Eleanor to conduct the National Symphony in Marjorie's honor at Constitution Hall. Surrounded by her three daughters and several grandchildren, and wearing a pink satin gown (fig. 205), the highlight of the evening was the Symphony's "Happy Birthday" serenade to its most important benefactress.[26] Over the years, Marjorie had donated $2 million to the National Symphony.[27]

She had co-founded the International Red Cross Ball in Palm Beach in 1957 and given her support ever since. The Red Cross Balls accounted for her most stellar appearances in the late 1960s. In 1967, she appeared in a blue dress complemented with a symphony of diamond and turquoise jewelry including a historic diadem that once belonged to Empress Marie Louise and is now in the Smithsonian National Museum of Natural History. In 1968, she was the belle of the ball, wearing a ruby tiara and ruby necklace to accent her Oldric Royce gown (see figs. 206, 207). Afterwards, she wrote to the designer and said, "I want to tell you that I wore the beautiful white dress with the black lace embroidery to the Red Cross Ball and it was greatly admired. It fit perfectly and I thoroughly enjoyed wearing it, and expect to wear it many times."[28]

By 1965, Marjorie had hopes of turning Mar-a-Lago into a Winter White House. She wanted to preserve her beloved mansion since her daughters had no interest in maintaining the 115-room estate. To do so would require approval by the Department of the Interior and the executive branch. Marjorie invited members of the House Interior Committee and their wives to visit her at Mar-a-Lago, and the Committee approved the idea. Next, she

invited Lady Bird Johnson and George Hartzog, Jr., director of the National Park Service, which would be responsible for maintaining the property, to tour her treasured estate. Lady Bird Johnson later referred to Mar-a-Lago in her memoir, *A White House Diary*, as "that beautiful never-never land."[29]

In 1968, Marjorie offered Hillwood to the Smithsonian Institution with the understanding that she could live there until she died. She wanted the exquisite collections she had amassed during her lifetime to be available for the public to enjoy. In January 1969, the regents of the Smithsonian ratified the agreement. In 1972, Marjorie's beloved Mar-a-Lago was declared a National Historical Landmark. She also planned to give Camp Topridge to the state of New York.[30]

"It has been my distinct pleasure to have been an interested observer throughout so many transitions … and to have had an active part in so many different eras," Marjorie said in Palm Beach in 1969.[31]

"I have been blessed with a variety of fascinating experiences," Marjorie told *Life* magazine. "It has been such an interesting life."[32]

To celebrate her eighty-third birthday in 1970, Marjorie invited ninety people to Mar-a-Lago for a dinner and dance party. Syndicated columnist Suzy wrote that Marjorie looked like a hundred million—for her that's easy—in a dear little peasant blouse with short sleeves and a deep ruffled neck, a flaring black velvet skirt embroidered in brilliants, her fabulous pearls, and a coral necklace. As she whirled and dipped in the tango (you go to Mrs. Post to dance or you stay home) her pleated red taffeta petticoat flashed and her red shoes twinkled. Wow! … Mrs. Post may well be the world's most beautiful and remarkable octogenarian.[33]

After leading a life that was a glamorous swirl of magnificent homes, exotic travel, rarified collections, elegant entertaining, and generous philanthropy, Marjorie Merriweather Post died peacefully in her sleep on September 12, 1973 at age eighty-six. Through the journey of her life, Marjorie had grown from an ingenue to an icon. As *Time* magazine said, "a gilt-edged volume of American history came to an end."[34]

205
Evening gown
Pink silk satin, cotton polyester lace, plastic ribbon
Oldric Royce, Inc., New York City, 1967
48.134
Marjorie looked pretty in pink when she wore her pale pink gown to celebrate her eightieth birthday (fig 204).

206
*Marjorie entering the Red Cross
Ball, escorted by Col. C. Michael
Paul and by a member of the U.S.
Marine Corps*
Palm Beach, Florida, 1968
Marjorie made a regal entrance in
this evening dress at the American
Red Cross Ball.

207
Evening dress
Cream and fuchsia raw silk, black
cotton lace, red plastic beads
Oldric Royce, Inc., New York City,
1968
48.135

208
Marjorie Merriweather Post at the Red Cross Ball
Palm Beach, Florida, 1968
Photograph: Bob Davidoff
Throughout her life Marjorie maintained her classic style and elegant manner of dressing.

209
Marjorie Post's closet in the bedroom suit at Hillwood Estate, Museum & Gardens

Endnotes

1   Nancy Rubin, *American Empress: The Life and Times of Marjorie Merriweather Post* (New York: Villard Books, 1995), 330.
2   Estella M. Chung, *Living Artfully: At Home with Marjorie Merriweather Post* (Washington, D.C.: Hillwood Museum and Gardens Foundation; London: D Giles Limited, 2013), 114.
3   Ibid., 115.
4   Rubin, *American Empress*, 308.
5   Ibid., 335–36.
6   Ibid., 336.
7   Dina Merrill, interview, June 6, 2006, Oral history, Hillwood Collection.
8   Rubin, *American Empress*, 335.
9   Gustav Modig, interview by Anne Odom and Liana Paredes Arend, February 5, 1999, Oral history, Hillwood Collection, 21.
10   Rubin, *American Empress*, 328.
11   Ibid., 341.
12   Ellen MacNeille Charles, interview by Stephanie Brown, November 13, 2003, Oral history, Hillwood Collection, 28.
13   Nettie Leitch Major, *C.W. Post, The Hour and The Man; A Biography with Genealogical Supplement* (Washington, D.C.: Judd & Detweiler, 1963), 198.
14   Teri Agins, *Wall Street Journal*, April 28, 1993, A12.
15   Chung, *Living Artfully*, 18.
16   "Milliner for Famous," *Washington Post*, February 7, 1977, C6.
17   Chung, *Living Artfully*, 94.
18   Sally Parker, "Martha Matilda Harper and the American Dream," https://www.rochester.edu/pr/Review/V63N1/feature2.html (accessed August 6, 2014).
19   Chung, *Living Artfully*, 94.
20   Ibid. 59.
21   Ibid. 111.
22   Betty Beale, *Power at Play: A Memoir of Parties, Politicians and the Presidents in My Bedroom*, 212.
23   Rubin, *American Empress*, 349.
24   Gustav Modig, interview by Anne Odom and Liana Paredes Arend, February 19, 1999, Oral history, Hillwood Collection, 37.
25   Rubin, *American Empress*, 360.
26   Ibid.
27   William Wright, *Heiress: The Rich Life of Marjorie Merriweather Post* (Washington, D.C.: New Republic Books, 1978), 241.
28   Marjorie Merriweather Post to Oldric Royce, February 9, 1968, Hillwood Collection.
29   Rubin, *American Empress*, 366–77.
30   Ibid., 368–69.
31   *Palm Beach Chronicle* 1, no. 1 (January 10, 1979).
32   "A World Unique and Magnificent," *Life*, November 4, 1965, 70.
33   Rubin, *American Empress*, 370.
34   *Time* (September 24, 1973).

Makers Glossary

B. Altman & Company (1865–1989) New York, NY; started as a dry goods store, Benjamin Altman turned it into a department store by 1888, establishing B. Altman & Company as a conservative, but leading NY clothier for many decades throughout major cities in the United States.

Au Bon Marché (est. 1838–present) Paris, France; originally founded as a small shop in 1838, the store reopened in 1850 to eventually become one of the oldest and best-known department stores in France, providing both mass-manufactured goods and high-end apparel.

Baker (est. 1892–1914) Washington, D.C.; a small dressmaker shop owned by the Baker sisters located in northwest Washington, D.C.

Bergdorf Goodman (est. 1901) New York, NY; White Plains, NY; established through the partnership of Edwin Goodman and Herman Bergdorf, the firm became well known as a women's specialty store. Bergdorf Goodman provided the latest ready-made fashion from European and American designers, making a name for itself as an exclusive department store.

Bob Shoes, Inc. (est. 1914–1971) New York, NY; Madame Bob, a custom bootier, established her shop just off the "Ladies Mile" and eventually moved it to Fifth Avenue.

Bonwit Teller (est. 1895–1990) New York, NY; created by Paul J. Bonwit and Edmund D. Teller, a specialty shop selling both imported and domestic apparel for women.

Callot Soeurs (est. 1895–1937) Paris, France; a leading couture house known for their feminine details and exotic influence. Callot Soeurs was managed by four sisters: Marie Callot Gerber, Marthe Callot Bertrand, Regina Callot Tennyson-Chantrell, and Josephine Callot Crimont. In 1928, Pierre Gerber, son of Marie Callot Gerber, took over the business.

Carnegie Ladies Hatter (1909–1918) New York, NY; see Hattie Carnegie.

Hattie Carnegie (1909–1976) New York, NY; originally established in 1909 as Carnegie Ladies Hatter, a dressmaking salon was established in 1918. Hattie Carnegie turned her shop into a reputable and well-known business providing some of the best made-to-order and ready-to-wear fashions, as well as jewelry and perfumes, by the 1920s and 1930s. In high demand for many decades, Hattie Carnegie was most known for her sophisticated attire and feminine suits. Carnegie never

sewed or designed for the shop, but relied on the aid of designers who would become well known in their own right.

Eaves Costume Company (est. 1863–1998) New York, NY; created by Albert Eaves, it was one of New York City's oldest and largest costume companies providing apparel and accessories for Broadway and major theatrical productions nationwide. The company was sold to Dodger Costumes Ltd., and continued under that company until closing in 2005.

Eleanora Garnett (ca. 1950s) Shanghai; Italy; New York, NY; a couturier of women's attire, known for her unique designs and personalized dresses. Her clothes were available at her store in New York as well as in Italy, where they were made in Rome on the Via de Villa Sacchetti.

Gervais Importers (ca. 1920s) New York, NY; small shop with predominantly custom-made versions of clothes by Chanel, Paquin, Patou, and Vionnet.

Hitchins & Baleow (ca. 1890–1910) New York, NY; custom-made dress shop.

J. & J. Slater (est. 1858–ca. 1945) New York, NY; established by James Slater and John J. Slater, J. & J. Slater was a manufacturer and retailer of footwear for women.

Charles James (1934–1939) Paris and (1940–1958) New York, NY; a fashion designer who worked with legendary couturiers in Paris and New York, his custom designs were known for being both sculptural and avant-garde.

Jay Thorpe (est. 1920s–closed 1970s) New York, NY; an exclusive salon known for their millinery apparel, Jay Thorpe operated as a department store offering clothing from both French and in-house designers.

Jay's Limited (est. 1906–present) London, England; a department store that provides women's fashions and the latest styles of dresses and apparel.

Esther Kirwan Steck (b. 1896–d. 1977) Washington, D.C.; milliner who created hats for the high society of Washington, D.C. during the mid-twentieth century.

Ann Lowe (1928–ca. 1970) New York, NY; a professional seamstress, who was commissioned as a designer for some of the major fashion houses in high-end New York department stores, Ann Lowe's clients included society's elite. Her one-of-a-kind dresses were known for their

trapunto, or quilt-like, stitching. Ann Lowe had her own fashion house on Madison Avenue between 1962 and 1970.

Lucile (est. 1891–1920s); London, England; New York, NY; Paris, France; Chicago, IL; the dressmaking business of Lady Duff Gordon (Lucy Sutherland) became one of the most successful and sought-after couture establishments in London (The Maison Lucile), New York (Lucile Ltd), Paris, and Chicago throughout the first few decades of the twentieth century. Lucile dresses and lingerie were widely popular and known for their romantic and feminine details.

Madame Frances (n.d.) New York, NY; a designer and custom dressmaker, named Frances Spingold, who worked for well-known clientele on both the East and West Coasts. Her firm specialized in romantic portrait dresses.

Madeleine & Madeleine (est. 1919–1925) Paris, France; well known in the 1920s, their styles were successful with American women interested in Parisian fashion. Capes and fringes were popular in their designs.

Martha, Inc. (1932–1992) New York, NY; Palm Beach, FL; salon that imported haute couture designs from Europe, especially Italy. Custom-made designs were created for select individuals and Martha, Inc. was one of the best-known firms at the time.

Oldric Royce, Inc. (1941–1965) New York, NY; Oldrich Rosenbaum was born in 1896 in Prague. He immigrated to the United States from Czechoslovakia in the late 1930s. In the United States, Mr. Rosenbaum changed his name to Oldric Royce and opened a successful fashion house providing made-to-order styles.

Orry-Kelly (1930s–1960s) Los Angeles, CA; costume designer best known for his Hollywood creations, Orry George Kelly designed fashions for a multitude of studios and all the top stars of the 1930s, '40s, and '50s.

Jeanne Paquin (est. 1891–present) Paris, France; the first woman to open her own fashion house, Paquin was known for her innovative designs. She produced eighteenth century-inspired dresses and sold a variety of evening attire at her Maison Paquin couture house in France, one of the largest in the country.

Victoria G. Petrini (b. 1897–d. 1993) Washington, D.C.; a seamstress and dressmaker who sewed for the high society of Washington, D.C. during the mid-twentieth century.

Robert Piguet (est. 1933–present) Paris, France; a designer who studied fashion under the top Parisian designers, Piguet founded his own fashion house in 1933 where he became known for his wearable and youthful, yet refined, fashions.

Pollak & Bruder (est. 1909) Vienna, Austria; a lady's fashion house on the Kohlmarkt, a shopping street in the first district of Vienna with international fashion labels.

Rosie Renault (est. 1919) New York, NY; born in Florence, Italy, established a dressmaking salon in Rome before moving her business to New York where she specialized in suits of fine tweed and woolens. She created clothing for New York society women and ladies of Broadway.

Rizik Bros. (est. 1908–present) Washington, D.C.; a well-known design boutique, it supplies high-end apparel, both in-house and designer labels, to those in the national capital.

Béla Ross of Oldric Royce, Inc. (est. 1966–1982) New York, NY; Béla Ross, designer, and Tony Abate, tailor, purchased Oldric Royce, Inc. from Oldric Royce. In 1988, Abate become the sole owner (see Oldric Royce, Inc.).

Saks Fifth Avenue (est. 1924–present) New York, NY; created by the partnership of Horace Saks of Saks & Company and Bernard Gimbel of Gimbel Bros. It was the first upscale department store to establish itself nationwide. The Fifth Avenue location opened in 1924 providing a range of luxury apparel and fashionable goods for decades.

Stein Uniform Co. (ca. 1935–1965) Baltimore, MD; ready-made uniforms with the motto "Serving Those Who Serve Humanity."

Stéphane (n.d.) Paris, France.

Thurn (early twentieth century) New York, NY; a well-established fashion house, Thurn supplied America with the latest Parisian designs and helped generate support for domestic creations.

Tipicano Mexicanos (n.d.) South America.

Toute Prête, Inc., (est. twentieth century) New York, NY; this firm sold negligees and lingerie created by Mlle Marie of the label "Mlle Marie Maison Française".

Town-Travel Wear (ca. 1940s–1950s) New York, NY; an in-house boutique at the Waldorf Astoria Hotel, it provided women's apparel in the latest fashions.

The White House (est. 1906–present) London, England; established by Jean Delliere, this store sells "whites" or ready-made undergarments, lingerie, and stockings.

Widoff (ca. 1890–1920) New York, NY; custom-designed clothing and high-end ready-to-wear garments that were sold in New York fashion houses and retailers such as Trun and Hickson.

Dress Terms

Etiquette of Dress
Marjorie Post changed four times a day throughout her life.

Dressing
Tailored robe ensemble worn in private, before dressing or after undressing.

Morning
Dress suitable for morning at home. Made to look smart even though the fabric could be inexpensive washable cotton.

Daytime
Tailored dress or two-piece suit consisting of a dress and matching jacket appropriate for business, town wear, luncheons, and lectures.

Afternoon
Suitable for "dressy" daytime social functions depending on the formality of the occasion; elaborate in style and fabric.

Dinner
Glorified afternoon costume, less formal than an evening dress, often long. Has a covered shoulder and long or short sleeves on either the dress or the jacket.

Evening
Dress worn after seven o'clock in the evening made of delicate or luxurious fabric with a low-cut neckline. These styles were worn to many types of events such as dinners, concerts, or the theatre.

Ball
Elaborate type of evening dress worn to formal social occasions.

Dance
Youthful, often bouffant in style with décolletage and usually sleeveless.

Ensemble
Two or more garments designed to be worn together in a harmonizing style, fabric or color.

Night
Designed to be worn in private at night, or any garment worn to bed.

Bibliography

Beale, Betty. *Power at Play: A Memoir of Parties, Politicians and the Presidents in My Bedroom*. Washington, D.C.: Regnery Gateway, 1993.

Benziger, Marieli, with the assistance of Rita Benziger. *August Benziger, Portrait Painter*. Glendale, CA: The Arthur H. Clark Company, 1958.

Black, J. Anderson, and Madge Garland. *A History of Fashion*, updated and revised by Frances Kennett. New York: William Morrow and Company, 1980.

Callan, Georgina O'Hara. *The Thames & Hudson Dictionary of Fashion and Fashion Designers*. London: Thames & Hudson, 1998.

Chung, Estella M. *Living Artfully: At Home with Marjorie Merriweather Post*. Washington, D.C.: Hillwood Museum and Gardens Foundation; London: D Giles Limited, 2013.

Lee, Sarah Tomerlin, ed. *American Fashion: The Life and Lines of Adrian, Mainbocher, McCardell, Norell, Trigère*. New York: Quadrangle, 1975.

Major, Nettie Leitch. *C.W. Post, The Hour and The Man; A Biography with Genealogical Supplement*. Washington, D.C.: Judd & Detweiler, 1963.

Papi, Stefano, and Alexandra Rhodes. *20th Century Jewelry & The Icons of Style*. London: Thames & Hudson, 2013.

Rubin, Nancy. *American Empress: The Life and Times of Marjorie Merriweather Post*. New York: Villard Books, 1995.

Salisbury, Frank O. *Portrait and Pageant* (1944), rev. as *Sarum Chase*. London: John Murray, 1953.

Wright, William. *Heiress: The Rich Life of Marjorie Merriweather Post*. Washington, D.C.: New Republic Books, 1978.

Index

Page numbers in italics indicate illustrations and their captions